AZTEC
WISDOM

AZTEC WISDOM

—

Timeless everyday healing techniques

SUZANNE EDWARDS

SIRIUS

To Bobby, a fellow lover of México
who now walks in the Michtlan.

All images courtesy of Shutterstock.

SIRIUS

This edition published in 2022 by Sirius Publishing, a division of
Arcturus Publishing Limited,
26/27 Bickels Yard, 151–153 Bermondsey Street,
London SE1 3HA

ISBN: 978-1-3988-1780-7
AD010237UK

Printed in China

Contents

Introduction

Aztec spirituality is rich and complex. Comprising a variety of ethnic groups that lived in central Mexico from the early 1300s to the early 1500s, the Aztecs took much of their culture from the Toltecs, their Mesoamerican predecessors, whom they revered. Aztecs were the masters of dreaming, and it was a dream that brought me to learn about this very tradition.

For no obvious reason, I have been strongly drawn to Mexico ever since I was a teenager. In 2013, I was visiting Chichén Itzá, the former site of a large Mayan city located on the Yucatán Peninsula, and I bought a piece of golden sheen obsidian. A couple of weeks later, I unwrapped it and lay it next to my bed as I slept. That night I had a dream that I can only describe as being in a white room and dancing with obsidian all

Obsidian rock crystal with a polished obsidian mirror

night. This is what I've come to realise is known as a "white dream" – a dream of spiritual instruction.

I knew the dream was significant, and felt that it meant I needed to somehow find work with obsidian. I decided to seek out a teacher that specialised in the rock – a shiny black material formed from melted lava – but I wanted someone Mexican. I'd heard of a tradition of a women's practice with an obsidian egg, but online searches led me nowhere. What I did find, however, was a link to an obsidian mirror workshop hosted in London by Sergio Magaña, a renowned Mexican shaman.

Of course, I went. And thus began my immersion into the tradition of scrying with obsidian mirrors. I'd heard that 16th-century occultist

Day of The Dead celebrations

and astronomer John Dee owned one – now in the possession of the British Museum – and I had also tried scrying with a crystal ball as a teenager, but I couldn't connect with the practice. This, however, was something totally different. It was complex, methodical and with a deep cosmology connected to everything that we were doing. At Sergio's workshop, we were not instructed to read the future inside this mirror like you might expect (though it can be used for that). Instead, we were introduced into an intricate system for deep self-development.

Sergio is down-to-earth and has a great sense of humour, coupled with humility and an encyclopaedic knowledge of the systems that he is working with. I knew that I was just at the beginning of a long journey – and, indeed, there was so much to learn. A whole array of dreaming practices, astrology and healing techniques, in fact. The full training of a *nahual* – a religious practitioner of the Mesoamerican region – takes 52 years. I have only just scratched the surface.

Sergio has had quite a few teachers himself, and I have had the privilege of encountering some of them. Listening to Hugo Nahui transmitting his wisdom in Mexico City, or Alma Santiago and her husband, Xolotl – in Devon, in south-west England, of all places! – are experiences I shall never forget.

Encountering the wisdom of the Aztec culture on actual sacred sites in Mexico was another thing entirely. The sites came alive, and I could see how the practices were designed to work synergistically with the temples the Aztecs had built. The power of this land was palpable. Despite attempts to repress and eradicate it, the magical nature of ancient Mexican culture can still be felt today, and witnessed at the Day of the Dead celebrations, through the huge popularity of the female deity Santa Muerte, and the Aztec dances and *limpia* cleansings that still happen today in the Zócalo, the famous square in Mexico City.

With a different perspective on the nature of reality, Aztec traditions offer profound wisdoms. There is much the whole world could learn about how we create our own reality through our dream life.

We create much of our own suffering and problems with our *yaotl*. This is our inner enemy or saboteur. It's the force inside us that seeks to destroy us. It is more obvious in some people than others, but we all have it, whether through self-destructive behaviour such as substance abuse or other harmful addictions, or creating troublesome relationships with friends and lovers. It can also express itself through financial mismanagement, or other negative patterns of behaviour. All of these things, in one way or another, shorten our existence.

The dreamwork, understanding of our astrological influences, and spiritual cleansing that Aztec traditions offer can all serve to keep our *yaotl* in check, minimising its power over us and giving us a stronger ability to create a more desirable reality. Learning to create synergy with the energies and deities that are more powerful than ourselves, and to live in harmony with the astrological calendar is a large part of the work of learning the Aztec traditions. If done well, we can live within the whirling ecosystems of these different forces and use them to our advantage. We will look at how you can use some of these practices in your modern day-to-day lives.

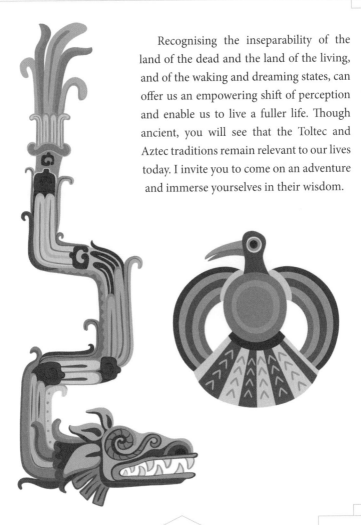

Recognising the inseparability of the land of the dead and the land of the living, and of the waking and dreaming states, can offer us an empowering shift of perception and enable us to live a fuller life. Though ancient, you will see that the Toltec and Aztec traditions remain relevant to our lives today. I invite you to come on an adventure and immerse yourselves in their wisdom.

CHAPTER 1

The myths and history of the Toltecs and Aztecs

The Toltecs

Considered the predecessors of the Aztecs, the Toltecs were alive from 900 to 1531, and their empire spanned over what are now the Tula and Hidalgo regions of Mexico. A lot of our information about the Toltecs come from the Aztecs, who held them in high esteem.

The Toltecs are said to have come from the Tolteca-Chichimeca people, who migrated from the north-west deserts to settle in Culhuacan, in the Valley of Mexico (which covers modern-day Mexico City and what was once Teotihuacan). Like the Aztecs, the Toltecs had also escaped from oppressive rulers when they established their capital in Tula. The city was destroyed by unknown forces in 1150, and the Toltecs' empire eventually crumbled. The site was subsequently looted by the Aztecs, and the remaining Toltecs resettled at Chapultepec ("Grasshopper Hill"), which is currently a large park in Mexico City.

Among their many sophistications, the Toltecs invented the Mesoamerican calendar. The Aztecs also claimed the Toltecs were master metallurgists and craftsmen, and that Tula was abundant with exquisite palaces made of jade, turquoise, gold and the feathers of the *quetzal*, the strikingly-coloured bird that is considered by many to be the most beautiful in the world. The Toltecs' craftsmanship had brought the city much wealth, as well as major trade in obsidian from the nearby Pachuca.

While still in Tula, the Toltecs made the first *chacmools*. These statues, which depict reclining figures resting on their elbows, with a bowl or disc on their abdomen, are believed by some scholars to depict fallen warriors, and that the vessels were used to hold sacrificial offerings. The Aztecs took on many of the Toltecs' religious practices and art, and even had an expression, "*toltecayotl*", which means "to have a Toltec heart" and to be deserving and exemplary in all that you do.

Toltec chacmool, National Museum of Anthropology, Mexico City

The Aztecs

The original name for the Aztec people is Mexica. The term "Aztec" was coined by Alexander von Humboldt, a German explorer who travelled the Americas in the early 1800s and took the name from the word "Aztlan".

Aztlan is the place where the Aztecs were said to have come from. It is unclear whether this was a literal place on Earth or a mythical land, but its name means "Place of the Heron" or "Place of Whiteness". (Note the similarity to the word "Atlantis", the lost city of Greek myth.)

There were seven tribes in Aztlan. When some of the rulers became tyrannical and abusive to their people, Huitzilopochtli, the god of the sun and of war, who is often represented as a hummingbird, began entering the dreams of the tribespeople. Showing them how to overcome their weakness to become the strongest tribe, Huitzilopochtli also instructed them to search for an eagle perched on a prickly pear cactus, eating a serpent – the sign that they had found a new homeland.

The Mexica people were said to have left Aztlan in 1064. They entered the Basin of Mexico around 1250. Finally, they found their symbol in Lake Texcoco, one of five interconnected lakes which formed the Aztec region, Anáhuac. Around 1325 they settled there and founded Tenochtitlan ("Among the Stone-Prickly Pear Cactus Fruit"). Now known as the historic part of Mexico City, Tenochtitlan was the capital of the Aztec Empire and home to the Templo Mayor, the Aztecs' main political and religious centre.

The empire included three city-states: Tenochtitlan, Tetzcoco and Tlacopan, a powerful alliance of self-governed lands with sophisticated systems of education (every child – boy and girl – from every walk of life had mandatory schooling), agriculture (various irrigation methods enabled diverse farming), artisan skills, calendar readings, medicine and science.

Both the Aztec and Toltec people spoke Nahuatl. A language that was used in Central Mexico since around the seventh century, it is to this day still spoken by up to 1.7 million Nahua people around Central America and the United States of America, with many words – such as chocolate (*cacahuatl*) and avocado (*ahuacatl*) – still in common use. Nahuatl is also considered by some to be a sacred language, with words that hold a lot of spiritual power, especially when spoken in a ceremonial context.

The Aztecs documented their lives in codices – pictorial manuscripts which have provided an important source of information about their lifestyles, ceremonies, history, scientific discoveries, property and land rights, particularly from the time before the Spanish Conquest. Because the Aztecs did not have an alphabet, their contents were mainly represented in pictographs – glyphs rather than lettered writing – which depicted events, objects and even sounds. Libraries full of codices were, however, destroyed by other indigenous leaders as they were collaborating with the Spanish to overthrow the Aztecs, who they viewed as their oppressors.

Huitzilopochtli, Aztec sun god

The Spanish Conquest and the end of the Aztec Empire

Differences in cultural perspectives, agendas and linguistics have given rise to many versions of the events that unfolded throughout the Spanish Conquest, so it is hard to be certain about exactly what occurred. Its beginnings, however, can be traced back to the early 1500s and the arrival in Mexico of the Spanish conquistador Hernán Cortés, whose expedition to Central America would ultimately lead to the Spanish colonisation of the Americas.

In 1521, Cortés arrived in the Aztec capital of Tenochtitlan. By that point, he had been in Mexico for two years, having first arrived in the Yucatán, where he landed with an army of approximately 630 men before gathering troops from other indigenous groups who were willing to become allies with the Spanish in order to overthrow the Aztecs. Anywhere between 10,000 and 20,000 Tlaxcalans joined up to fight, in order to rescue their tribes from paying tax to the Aztecs. But the Aztecs weren't willing to let go without a fight.

En route to Tenochtitlan, Cortés and his men travelled through Cholula, a large Aztec city that housed the largest pyramid in the world: a temple to Quetzalcoatl, the feathered serpent. The Spanish were allowed to enter and stay in the city but, as enemies of the Aztecs, the

Tlaxcalans were ordered to stay outside the city boundaries. Rumours of a Cholulan attack began to spread throughout the Spanish camp, and two noblemen were able to confirm that an ambush was being planned for when they left the city.

Cortés confronted the locals in front of the temple of Quetzalcoatl, and the Cholulans did not deny the plot, claiming they were only

Hernán Cortés enters Cholula

carrying out the orders of Moctezuma II, ruler of the Aztec Empire. Cortés fired a shot from his musket, initiating a bloody combat in which 3,000 Cholulans – ten per cent of the city's population – were killed and the city left in ruins. Cortés then declared that he would march on Tenochtitlan as a conqueror. Though Moctezuma II denied any involvement in the ambush, the tone for what would follow had already been set.

CORTÉS: MAN OR GOD?

A popular theory has it that that the Aztecs believed Cortés to be Quetzalcoatl incarnate, as the Spanish conquistador's arrival coincided with a specific date, predicted by astrologists, that their god would arrive from the east.

This has since been debated. On Cortés' arrival, Moctezuma II refused to meet him, sending tributes instead. This idea would have also been dispelled by Cortés' destruction of Cholula, a site dedicated to the serpent-god himself.

MOCTEZUMA II: GENEROUS OR COWARDLY?

Instead of meeting Cortés, who by July 1519 had assumed control of Veracruz, in eastern Mexico, Moctezuma II sent instead gifts of gold, mother-of-pearl and obsidian mirrors, which was a common way to solve disputes in Mesoamerican society. As Cortés' interest in gold became clear, Moctezuma sent more of it, including a six-and-a-half foot gold wheel and a helmet filled with gold dust. After forming an alliance with the Tlaxcalans, he received treasure from them as well. With the king of Spain, Charles V, showing signs of withdrawing his support of Cortés' exhibition, Cortés sent him a fifth of the riches he had earned, in order to regain favour.

Proclaiming himself an ambassador of Charles V, Cortés managed to negotiate entrance into Tenochtitlan, where Moctezuma II met him on the causeway into the city. Receiving further precious gifts – discs of the Aztec calendar, in gold and silver – Cortés had them melted down for their metals.

According to the *Florentine Codex*, a Nahuatl study written in the 16th century by the Spanish Franciscan friar Bernardino de Sahagún, Moctezuma II bowed his head very low to Cortés and said:

Moctezuma II

'Our lord, you are very welcome in your arrival in this land. You have come to satisfy your curiosity about your noble city of Mexico. You have come here to sit on your throne, to sit under its canopy, which I have kept for a while for you. For the rulers and governors [of past times] have gone: Itzcoatl, Moctezuma I, Axayacatl, Tiçocic, and Ahuitzotl. [Since they are gone], your poor vassal has been in charge for you, to govern the city of Mexico. Will they come back to the place of their absence? If even one came, he might witness the marvel that has taken place in my time, see what I am seeing, as the only descendent of our lords. For I am not just dreaming, not just sleepwalking, not seeing you in my dreams. I am not just dreaming that I have seen you and have looked at you face to face. I have been worried for a long time, looking toward the unknown from which you have come, the mysterious place. For our rulers departed, saying that you would come to your city and sit upon your throne. And now it has been fulfilled, you have returned. Go enjoy your palace, rest your body. Welcome our lords to this land.'

Cortés replied:

> 'Tell Moctezuma to not be afraid, for we greatly esteem
> him. Now we are satisfied because we have seen him
> in person and heard his voice. For until now, we have
> wanted to see him face to face. And now we have seen
> him, we have come to his home in Mexico, slowly he
> will hear our words.'

There are various opinions about what this exchange means. One is that this was a fictionalised account of the meeting, fabricated by the Spanish in order to give the impression that Moctezuma II was willing to hand over the Aztec Empire to what he believed was the human incarnation of the feathered serpent Quetzalcoatl.

However, another theory is that Nahuatl is an almost overly polite language, and that Moctezuma II actually meant the opposite of what he was saying, which would have been a Nahuatl way of conveying superiority.

There is also a third idea that, as Moctezuma II was a master of dreams and prophecy (as expected of an Aztec ruler), he knew what was coming before the Spanish did – indeed, that he had prophesied it ten years earlier, after interpreting a comet sighting as an omen that his empire would soon end. Other premonitions came in the shape of babies being born with deformities, and a fire in the temple of Huitzilo-

Ruins of temple of Huitzilopochtli in Tenochtitlan

pochtli, the sun god who had led the Aztecs to their homeland. The fire would not go out and any attempts to douse the flames only made it burn stronger.

Some scholars have perceived Moctezuma II's offerings to Cortés to be cowardly, or a sign of bad leadership. But it could also be said that it took wisdom on his part to accept there was something at work which was beyond his control and desires, and to resist it would result in more suffering and bloodshed.

Cortés and his people were given quarters to stay in. One of the soldiers, Bernal Díaz del Castillo, later recorded the many marvels of the city of Tenochtitlan.

'When we saw so many cities and villages built in
the water and other great towns on dry land we were
amazed and said that it was like the enchantments [...]
on account of the great towers and cues and buildings
rising from the water, and all built of masonry. And
some of our soldiers even asked whether the things that
we saw were not a dream? [...] I do not know how to
describe it, seeing things as we did that had never been
heard of or seen before, not even dreamed about.'

Within a week of Cortés's arrival, Moctezuma II was taken captive
but ordered to continue to "rule" under Spanish orders, so that the
Aztec Empire would not be cut off from supplies. He complied, but
resentment was growing among the Aztec people.

Death of Moctezuma II and fall of Tenochtitlan

Moctezuma II's death is the cause of some speculation, including
one story that a younger brother, Cuitláhuac, secretly ordered his
assassination. Another has it that the ruler was killed in an attack on his
palace, after he had been forced by the Spanish to order rebellious Aztec

warriors to refrain from battling the Spaniards. Bernal Díaz del Castillo later recalled that Moctezuma II died after receiving three wounds – to the head, arm and leg – from stones launched by furious Aztecs.

With Moctezuma II dead, Cortés realised he could not hold Tenochtitlan any longer. On 30 June 1520 – the "Night of Sorrows" – the Spaniards tried to sneak out of the city under the cover of darkness but were spotted. Six hundred of Cortés's men – about half of his army – were killed, and the Spanish retreated from the city. They had, however, left a deadly threat behind.

Many of the deceased soldiers had fallen into Tenochtitlan's lagoon, infecting the water with smallpox. Though the Spanish were immune to the disease, the indigenous population had never encountered it before: when the Aztec warriors bathed their wounds in the lagoon's water, they became infected. Half the population of Tenochtitlan died of the disease – with Cuitláhuac reportedly the first to perish – hugely reducing Aztec defences.

Cuauhtémoc, a nephew and son-in-law of Moctezuma II, became the Aztecs' next ruler. According to oral tradition, he concentrated on hiding their knowledge, codices and sacred stones from the Spanish, including in the nearby sites of Teotihuacan and Tula.

Shortly before the fall of Tenochtitlan, Cuauhtémoc gave the following speech:

"Our sun has gone down in darkness.

Monument to Cuitláhuac, Mexico City

It is a sad evening for Tenochtitlan, Texcoco, Tlatelolco.

The moon and the stars are winning this battle,

Leaving us in darkness and despair.

Let's lock ourselves up in our houses,

Let's leave the paths and the marketplaces deserted,

Let's hide deep in our hearts our love for the codices, the ball game, the dances, the temples,

Let's secretly preserve the wisdom that our honourable grandparents taught us with great love,

And this knowledge will pass from parents to children, from teachers to students,

Until the rising of the Sixth Sun,

When the new wise men will bring it back and save Mexico.

In the meantime, let's dance and remember the glory of Tenochtitlan,

The place where the winds blow strongly."

Cortés took several months to regroup, and returned to Tenochtitlan with 800 conquistadores and tens of thousands of indigenous warriors willing to fight the Aztecs. They held the city under siege for 93 days until the Aztecs surrendered, on 13 August 1521. Much of the city had been looted or burned to the ground, and the Spaniards continued to destroy it after the Aztecs had surrendered. They then built what is now Mexico City on the site where Tenochtitlan once stood.

Human sacrifice: fact or myth?

When many people think of the Aztecs, they often picture gruesome images of still-beating hearts being ripped out of chests by terrifying warrior priests resplendent in large-feathered headdresses. Indeed, Bernal Diaz del Castillo relayed the Spanish conquistadors' shock at the intensity and volume of the sacrifices.

'Hardly a day passed by that these people did not sacrifice from three to four, and even five Indians, tearing the hearts out of their bodies, to present them to the idols and smear blood on the walls of the temple. The arms and legs of these unfortunate beings were then cut off and devoured, just in the same way we should fetch meat from a butcher's shop and eat it: indeed I even believe that human flesh is exposed for sale cut up in their markets.'

Just as they had interpreted Moctezuma II's welcome speech as an invitation to claim the Aztec Empire as their own, the Spanish drew on the Aztecs' use of human sacrifice as a justification for their conquering and treatment of the indigenous people. Cortés was well known for saying that one of the main reasons Charles V had sent him to Mexico was to abolish human sacrifice and the other "evil" rites the Aztecs practised.

Some historians and spiritual practitioners of the Aztec traditions have, however, suggested that the Spanish exaggerated their accounts, and that the volume of sacrifices carried out was a lot lower than reported. As Cortés clearly set out to conquer their land and take control of the Aztecs' wealth, it is difficult to know how trustworthy the Spanish accounts are. Some scholars have even come to believe that the Aztecs never even practised human sacrifice, and that the claims are lies that were intended to demonise the Aztec people and their culture.

TZOMPANTLIS

A major archaeological discovery, known as the Hueyi Tzompantli, has fuelled this debate. *Tzompantlis* are displays of human skulls, arranged as walls or towers, which were a feature in Aztec temples. Uncovered in 2017, in the archaeological zone of Templo Mayor, in Mexico City, Hueyi Tzompantli is five metres in diameter and contains 676 skulls. In its original form, it was made of seven 36-metre walls.

Many historians claim that the most obvious explanation for *tzompantlis* is that they were built to house the skulls of victims of sacrifice, either as a trophy wall, or a way of warding off invaders. There may, however, be other reasons for their existence. The word "*tzompantli*" also means "altar of skulls"; as passed down through the oral tradition, it has been said that the skulls on display belonged to the most powerful medicine people, warriors and rulers of the tribes. The altars were believed to have contained their vibrations, and visitors were said to have taken in the vibrations of these highly evolved beings that lived exemplary lives. Every Aztec family in the pre-colonial era had a skull altar, mostly featuring the skulls of their ancestors.

Tzompantlis also served to provide spiritual protection. Arranged to face inwards and outwards, rows of skulls imbued with the spirits of disciplined and courageous warriors forged a formidable defence against malevolent spirits entering the temple.

Tzompantlis are often written about in sensationalist language, but it is easy to forget that there are sites in other parts of the world – mainly Europe, but also Egypt and Peru, and nearly all churches – that contain human remains. Few, if any, of these are attributed to human sacrifice, but rather gather remains left behind from war, plagues and the actions of religious martyrs. Some of these date from more recent times than the Aztec Empire.

Like the Toltecs before them, the Aztecs had a profound, sophisticated and complex culture that sometimes overlapped with that of their predecessors. This culture has been misrepresented and suppressed since colonisation took place, but greater knowledge is progressively coming to the surface, giving the world a better understanding of the Aztecs' true beliefs.

Tzompantli, Mayan skull altar, Templo Mayor Museum

CHAPTER 2

The four Tezcatlipocas and the seven energy centres

F our – or *Nahui* in Nahuatl – is an important and sacred number in the Aztec tradition. In the Toltec creation myth, we start first with the Black Eagle or *Amomati* – the void, as Taoists would call it, or the darkness from which the light came in the Bible. In order to create, the Black Eagle became aware of its own reflection and started to look at it. This manifested as Tezcatlipoca, whose name in the Nahuatl language is often translated as "smoking mirror". It is worth noting that these beings are often referred to as deities but many practitioners of the tradition consider them to be essences or energies rather than Gods. I will use the terms interchangeably throughout the book – you can make up your own mind about what you prefer.

In turn, the "smoking mirror" then reflected a pair of Aztec deities, Ometecuhtli and Omecihuatl, known as Mr and Mrs Two. They are a couple – the male and female energies and essences. Often represented by the male figure blowing the conch and the female woman burning copal, a tree resin, the couple had four children – the four Tezcatlipo-cas – which all correlate to a different direction. Each Tezcatlipoca is an essence and has particular significance in different types of spiritual work. In the Toltec cosmology, each of the four were regarded as a petal on the same flower.

OMETEOTL

Before going into the four directions, it's important to mention "*Ometeotl*". This is a fundamental concept in the Aztec tradition and it is a word of power. You will hear it said at the end of every prayer and every ceremony. It's the Nahuatl equivalent of "Amen", "So mote it be" and even "Om".

It comes from the Nahuatl words "*ome*", meaning "two" and "*teotl*" meaning "energy". This word can move the 13 heavens and nine underworlds and the four directions – the flower that is representative of the universe. It represents duality – two forces coming together to create a new reality. It signifies the physical manifestation of a creation coming from the subtle world. As above, so below.

Brothers Quetzalcoatl, left, and Tezcatlipoca, right

NORTH: THE BLACK TEZCATLIPOCA

The first to be born was the Black Tezcatlipoca, corresponding with the north petal of the flower. Connected to the dream world, the same place as the land of the dead, the Black Tezcatlipoca governs the realm of the underworlds, the shadows and our caves. It is associated with the new moon, midnight and the autumn equinox.

This direction is used for work with our unconscious shadow, our repetitive problems, working with our ancestors or ancestral issues, and dreams. It is also for the removal of unwanted energies.

WEST: THE RED TEZCATLIPOCA

The Red Tezcatlipoca, the west petal, was the second to be born. Also known as Xipe Totec, this direction is for shedding, renewal and feminine energy. It's about getting rid of what you do not need in order to change and regenerate into what you want to become next. It also activates the dreams of the Black Tezcatlipoca and is associated with the sunset, the waning moon and the spring equinox.

SOUTH: THE BLUE TEZCATLIPOCA

The Blue Tezcatlipoca, of the south petal, was the third to be born. This was also the realm of Huitzilopochtli, the warrior hummingbird deity that led the Aztecs to Tenochtitlan, the capital of the Empire. Concerned with a place of repetitive patterns in the cosmos and also in ourselves, the Blue Tezcatlipoca guides us to gain the discipline of a warrior, so that that we might repeat patterns that serve us (for instance, in spiritual practice or that of a musical instrument) and drop negative habits and addictions that hold us back, so we can reach our highest potential. Like the Aztecs, he can guide us through our dreams. We can also learn prophecy here. The Blue Tezcatlipoca rules the dawn, the crescent moon and the winter solstice.

Huitzilopochtli

EAST: THE WHITE TEZCATLIPOCA

Lastly, we have the White Tezcatlipoca of the east petal, which is ruled by Quetzalcoatl. This is the place of light, precious knowledge and enlightenment. He rules midday, the full moon and the autumn equinox.

We will see four movements in many of the spiritual practices in the Aztec tradition, which represent the completion of the four Tezcatlipocas. First, the cleansing and facing of the underworlds and our shadow, followed by a shedding of what's unnecessary, which also allows us to renew. Next comes the strengthening of our discipline and the improvement of our actions and habits, guided by prophetic dreams. Finally, we evolve by filling ourselves with higher knowledge and wisdom and take steps towards fulfilling our greatest destiny.

The seven energy centres

The seven energy centres bear a striking resemblance to the seven main chakras in yoga. The word for them, "*totonalcayo*", means heat-producing spot.

COLOTL

Meaning "scorpion" in Nahuatl, the *colotl* is situated in the coccyx, right at the bottom of the spine. Working with and clearing this centre helps us to move forward and not remain stuck in "old winds", or repeated ancestral and past life patterns. Its colour is black.

IHUITL

This is the sexual centre, in the area of the genitals. It means feather because the idea is to keep the energy here light so that it can rise up through all of the centres. That said, heavy energy can be released here. *Coatzin* – or

Yogic chakras

the serpent, our sexual energy – builds whatever we create. We can ask ourselves: what do we want to create? Joy or suffering? Working with this centre ensures we keep our creations positive. The colours here are red and white.

PANTLI

Meaning "flag", this centre is in your belly button. Its colour is white. It's a reference to the number 20 and the 20 glyph signs that are central to Aztec astrology (we will go into this in more detail later). Each glyph sign is also combined with a number, which is called our *tonalli*. This is central to the lessons we need to work with and our potential.

For instance, my *tonalli* is 12 Cozcacuahtli (Necklace Eagle). When unbalanced it will attract "heavy" situations and wisdom will be gained in a hard way. On the hand, when it's in balance, wisdom will be given and received in a lighter way.

Working with this centre to keep it clear and light will help you cultivate the best qualities of your *tonalli*, even without knowledge of the glyph and number.

XOCHITL

This centre – which means "flower" – is a central meeting point of the different dualities: light and dark; past and future; heart and mind; body and spirit. If we learn to balance all these and release the heavy energies of our ancestors here, we can blossom and flourish with beauty in life. Otherwise, we will feel sorrow in our hearts. The colour here is red.

TOPALLI

The centre, which means "sceptre", is in the throat, the place of personal power. The colour is blue. We work on this centre to recover power – there are so many situations in life where we lose it, where others belittle us, where we perceive ourselves as having failed. We should also think about how we wield our power, as we can also use it destructively ourselves. Being fully empowered and using our power to create is a sign that this centre is in balance.

CHALCHIUHUITL

Meaning "jade" – the most precious substance to the Aztecs – this centre is located on the forehead. The colour for this centre is green, of course. The emotions are believed to be here – and when our emotions and this centre are in a balanced state, it can take us to "the place of paradise" – the bliss state. It is the point of union between the *nahual* and *tonal* – the two energy bodies key to our dream states, which we'll look at more closely in the next chapter.

TECPATL

Located at the crown of the head, this centre means "flint". It is also known as "the Knife of Justice", a centre whose main theme is karma. These are energetic flints on the crown of the head that can be seen by those with clairvoyant abilities. Some are dark and some are white. The dark ones are our negative karmic patterns that cause us repetitive problems; the bright ones are our positive karma, our gifts and talents.

XAYAXOLOHTLI

Exercise to raise your energy

Here is an exercise to help raise your energy up through your *totonalcayos*. Again, there are parallels with the yogic traditions and Kundalini energy, which, when unawakened, is depicted as a serpent coiled at the bottom of the spine. It can be awakened with different practices. In this tradition, the Aztecs would have referred to it as the Quetzalcoatl energy which is a feathered, or flying, serpent.

This exercise is particularly relevant to our times – the Sixth Sun, which is the return of Quetzalcoatl. Regular practice can bring about powerful transformation to you and your life, raising your energy and changing your karma.

* Sit facing east, in the direction of Quetzalcoatl.

* Inhale through your nose. Hold your breath. Visualise the serpent that is coiled at your coccyx moving up through all of your centres. You will be retaining your breath until the snake reaches your crown.

* As it moves through your coccyx/*colotl*, feel how you are healing your ancestral patterns.

* As it travels through your genital area/*ihuitl*, you are making your energy lighter.

* As it moves to your navel/*pantli*, you are exhibiting the best aspects of your birth chart and creating the changes you want in your life with ease.

* At your heart centre/*xochitl*, your whole being is flowering.

* At the centre of your forehead, the jade chakra/*chalchiuhuitl*, tonal and nahual are uniting.

* Finally at the crown/*tecpatl*, spin the snake around the crown of your head changing your destiny to unite with the precious knowledge and then exhale.

* Repeat 12 times.

* The 13th time, instead of simply spinning it, on the exhalation see yourself coming out through your crown in the form of a flying serpent.

* Next you have a choice: you can either transform from the snake into your favourite bird or follow the original technique, which is to turn into a quetzal bird and fly to the sun.

* See yourself reaching the sun and ask to receive the precious knowledge and transform into Quetzalcoatl.

* Put your hands together in a prayer position and say:

> *"Ometeotl. May life and precious knowledge bloom inside me. Ometeotl."*

As with all of the exercises, the more you practise this, the more benefits you will reap.

CHAPTER 3

Dream Work

Dreams are a driving force in the Mexican traditions. It is said that nothing that happens in waking life can occur unless it has been dreamed first. The chair you are sitting on and the device or physical book on which you are reading these words were all dreamed of before they came into existence.

All of the leaders and warriors would have been trained as master dreamers in order for them to have the self-mastery to lead and act with power and wisdom. Their dreams would have given them deep vision and insight, and they would have been trained to understand their significance.

It is thought the word Mexico comes from the Nahuatl words "*metzli*" and "*xictli*", meaning moon and navel – the navel of the

Dream state

moon. It is the land of the dreamers – and those who are awake whilst dreaming, which is to say lucid dreaming.

Lucid dreaming is a practice that involves training yourself to remain conscious and aware whilst dreaming – much like being awake – although there are some lucky people who can do it naturally. It has become extremely popular in recent years, but the Mexicas approached it differently.

In today's lucid dreaming, though there are sometimes aims or goals, it is often quite "freestyle" – the dreamer might change his or her clothes or decide to go skydiving, for example. With the Mexica practices there is more of a focus – one could even describe it as being methodical for the purposes of self-mastery, manifestation, healing and training for death.

REMEMBERING YOUR DREAMS

The most important step, albeit a simple one, is to begin by remembering your dreams. This helps take you from the state of unconscious to conscious dreaming. The less conscious you are of your dreams, the less conscious and in control you are of your waking state.

Before going to sleep at night simply state to yourself that you intend to remember your dreams. You can do this several times in your head. Keeping a dream journal is also recommended. Simply by giving more attention to your dream life you will begin to remember and engage with it more.

Tonal and Nahual

There are two energy bodies that are key to our dream states: *tonal* and *nahual*. In the waking state, the *tonal* surrounds our head. It is related to our personality, mind, the five senses, time and space, identity and the sun. When people have highly developed extrasensory perception, it creates an amber aura around the head – think of the halos around saints and angels, for example.

The *nahual*, in the waking state, is around our abdomen and is engaged when we are asleep. It's one of the energy bodies we use in death – it is who you are beyond your mind and material reality: who you *really* are. In the dream state, the two swap places, which is what allows us to dream. It is important for these two centres to be in harmony with each other, otherwise problems can occur.

THE NAVEL

In the Aztec tradition, it was considered important to have a strong abdomen, which gave the person more energy to dream. There are various types of posture or *quin*, which means "protector", that, when practised with specific breathwork, can help to cultivate a strong abdomen. I recommend practising these three as a set.

QUIN FOR THE TONAL

* Lie flat on your back.

* Make your intention to heal or balance your *tonal*.

* Raise your left leg. (It can be bent, straight or supported by a wall, the most important thing is to concentrate on using and strengthening your abdomen.)

* Face left and do nine sets of strong inhalations and exhalations – in through the nose and out through the mouth. (I recommend using your fingers to keep count of the number.)

* Face right and do another nine sets, breathing in the same way.

* Face up to the heavens and do another nine sets. (Be careful not to strain your neck.)

* Face your navel and do another nine sets.

* Lie back flat on the floor and take a moment to feel and integrate the energies.

QUIN FOR THE NAHUAL

* Lie flat on your back.

* Make your intention to heal or balance your *nahual*.

* Raise your right leg. (It can be bent, straight or supported by a wall, as above; again, the aim is to strengthen the abdomen.)

* Face left and do nine sets of strong inhalations and exhalations – in through the nose and out through the mouth.

* Face right and do another nine sets, breathing in the same way.

* Face up to the heavens and do another nine sets. (Be careful not to strain your neck.)

* Face your navel and do another nine breathing sets.

* Lie back flat on the floor and take a moment to feel and integrate the energies.

QUIN TO BALANCE YOUR TONAL AND NAHUAL

* Lie flat on your back.

* Make your intention to harmonise your *tonal* and *nahual*.

* Raise both your legs. (Again, they can be bent, straight, supported by a wall. The most important thing is to concentrate on strengthening your abdomen.)

* Face left and do nine sets of strong inhalations and exhalations – in through the nose and out through the mouth.

* Face right and do another nine sets, breathing in the same way.

* Face up to the heavens and do another nine sets. (Be careful not to strain your neck.)

* Face your navel and do another nine sets.

* Lie back flat on the floor and take a moment to feel and integrate the energies.

BALANCING YOUR SEXUAL ENERGY

Sexual energy is an essential source of power to fuel our dream work, but we dissipate it in so many ways: stress, negative emotions, overthinking, conflict, addictions and illness. This is why so many people struggle to cultivate a powerful and lucid dream life. Bringing awareness to this issue helps, but the Mexicas had specific techniques to work on their sexual energy as well. The exercise opposite can help heal and balance your sexual energy so you can put it to better use in your dream life.

It is important to generate, balance and heal our energies, otherwise we cannot become conscious and create accordingly in the dream state, or we potentially create more destruction and disharmony. I recommend practising dream recall and the exercises above with a view to healing and building up your energies before going on to the next stage of dream planting.

PIPITLIN AND YEYELLIS

Pipitlin and *yeyellis* are beings that feed from us, like angels and demons. The *yeyelli*s feed from negative emotions, such as anger, fear and sadness; the *pilpitlin* feed from happy emotions. In the Aztec tradition, in our dream state we sink to underworlds filled with *yeyelli*s, who feed off our suffering and draw us again and again into our problems, stories and ancestral negative patterns. This is the spiritual path of the Mexicas: to heal ourselves so we don't continually return to these underworlds, perpetually creating more suffering and limitations

CUETZPALIN (LIZARD) QUIN

* Lie face down on the floor

* Hold yourself up on your forearms and your right foot (if possible).

* Bend your left leg with your knee pointing outwards and pull your left foot as near to your groin as possible

* Face left and do nine sets of strong inhalations and exhalations – in through the nose and out through the mouth.

* Face right and do another nine sets, breathing in the same way.

* Face up to the heavens and do another nine sets. (Be careful not to strain your neck.)

* Face your navel and do another nine sets.

* Lie flat on the floor and take a moment to feel and integrate the energies.

for ourselves. It's what some modern spiritual practitioners would refer to as the Matrix. *Pilpitlin* can be encountered in the heavens, which we reach by travelling upwards in the dreamscape. They can be perceived as geometric shapes – think of sacred geometry. Although these beings feed from us – they're obviously preferable to the *yeyellis*! To become a true Nahual, the highest training involves transcending these two polarities. It takes 52 years of training, but it means you are no longer anyone's "food" and that you are truly in control of your life and consciousness.

Mexicatzin

Now we are going to do a special exercise for planting dreams. To do this, first you have to decide on what result you are aiming for. You are looking to turn your *nahual* into an animal form, which is why such forms are known as *nahuales*. This exercise should be done sitting up before sleeping. Here is a selection but there are many.

TOCHTLI

This is the rabbit, a *nahual* of the moon. It's a great one for dreamwork, fertility, abundance and creativity. The rabbit also has a 28-day reproductive cycle, similar to the lunar cycle; it can bring you favours from the moon.

TOCATL

The spider is the *nahual* of the collective. Like the worldwide web, it connects people, communities, ideas and countries. It's suitable for any situation where there are different people or factors involved. A web also catches things, of course.

HUITZILI

The hummingbird is a powerful *nahual* to work with as it's the warrior who makes the impossible possible. It's ideal for any situation where you need an extra boost of strength or willpower and it seems like you have a lot to achieve. The hummingbird is also for bringing about prophetic dreams, finding love and healing relationships. It's usually blue, but for love or relationships it's green.

ITZPAPALOTL

This is the obsidian or black butterfly. It's a special spirit that can take problems away, so if you want something removed completely from your life, like a sickness or a difficult problem, this is a good choice.

COATL

The snake is for physical healing and wisdom. Snakes are universally linked to medicine. The caduceus – the staff of Hermes, entwined by two serpents – is one of the most famous examples. If snakes bite the area that needs healing in a dream, this is a good sign. If it's a condition without a specific location, then ask the snake in your dream to bite your stomach.

CIPACTLI

The crocodile, or *cipactli*, represents Mother Earth and is great for manifesting all forms of abundance.

ITZCUINTLI

The dog is the *nahual* of the dead – it's the spirit that helps you to communicate and work with your ancestors to heal the bloodlines and your family (see Chapter 7 on death). Remember if you meet your ancestors in a dream, it's only truly them if their eyes are red.

EXERCISE

Once you have decided what you want to achieve, we will be doing cycles of 13 breaths, which are very similar to the *quin* exercises.

* Sitting up, face to the left. Do a cycle of 13 strong breaths (inhaling through the nose and exhaling through the mouth), holding the intention of destroying the opposite of what you want to create. For example, if you want to create passing an exam, then destroy failing the exam.

* Face to the right, doing a cycle of 13 breaths, destroying the dreams that are creating, or could create, any problems or setbacks.

* Face upwards and do a cycle of 13 breaths to destroy all the cosmic energy creating problems with this issue.

* Face downwards into your navel and do a cycle of 13 breaths. Visualise a bowl of water or an obsidian mirror there and that you are destroying your reflection with the breaths until it disappears.

* Face forwards and do a cycle of 13 breaths, holding your abdomen in as you exhale.

* After you have done the five cycles, visualise your chosen *nahual* inside your navel and moving up towards your chest or heart.

* Exhale and imagine you are breathing the nahual out of your chest and feel it moving to the right.

Repeat these words either in your head or out loud: "I am a dream warrior. I find myself lucid in my dreams in the form of the rabbit/serpent/[name your animal], bringing me fertility/healing of my back/[specify your request] and I'll find the dreams that I've sowed. *Mah Tocuenmanahcan* (Ma toc-qwen-mana-can) or 'May my intentions remain planted in my dreams'."

This whole sequence needs to be repeated four times, as, in this tradition, the number four represents a complete cycle in nature. Numbers are important.

You can use the same *nahual* with different, or the same, intentions, or you can choose four different *nahuales*. It's up to you how you do this.

After the fourth round, keep on repeating over and over: "I am a dream warrior..." as this will affirm your intention as you are falling asleep. It's a type of self-hypnosis, which trains your mind to create these dreams and become lucid.

Tip

If you are finding it hard to become lucid or find these *nahuales* in your dreams, there is a technique you can use, which involves waking up in the middle of the night between 3am and 4am, doing this exercise and going back to sleep. Breaking your night's sleep increases your chances of lucidity because of the brainwave patterns you go through during the sleep cycle.

The Mexica
language of dreams

Dream language – and the decoding of dreams – is hugely extensive in the Aztec tradition. I will give you a range of things to look out for, but this is just scratching the surface! It is often specific features and directions of movement that are key to what the dream signifies, rather than the enjoyment or fun factor. This is worth bearing in mind when examining your dreams.

COLOURS

Blue: Dreams in this colour are dreams of future events.

Green: This is the colour of emotional wellbeing.

Red: When you dream in red, physical healing and rejuvenation are possible. If you are lucid, you can request specific areas that need healing.

White: White in dreams will bring you spiritual information, instructions about ritual, ceremonies, sacred sites and healings.

DIRECTIONS

East: This is a benevolent direction. Anything moving to the right tends to bring a lighter, more positive outcome.

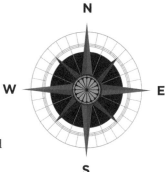

West: This is the direction of shedding and loss. Things moving to the left mean that the lessons ahead will be harder and suffering is likely.

North: Known as the direction of the dead, north is the direction we always face, to some extent, in our dreams. Anything that goes into this direction is going to end or change in some way.

South: It is this direction which brings dreams of the future. Some people have a tendency to face south often in dreams.

Down: As mentioned earlier, this direction takes you into the underworlds. It is preferable not to do this, especially if you are not lucid. There are some situations where it is done deliberately but that is for advanced practitioners – generally speaking, for the layperson, it is to be avoided.

Up: This direction takes us up to the heavens and brings us positivity, inspiration and beauty. If you have the opportunity, go upwards as much as possible!

ELEMENTS

Fire: The presence of fire means something is being destroyed, which can be welcome or unwelcome, depending on what it is – for example, whether it is abundance or a disease being destroyed! Smoke represents a transformation.

Water: Flat waters such as rivers, lakes, swimming pools are a sign of emotional trouble. Rain is a very welcome sight in a dream as it signifies purification and healing.

Earth: Dreams of violence and conflict between people are an indication that you are at war with the Earth. Conversely, dreams of

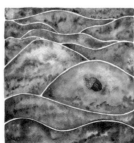
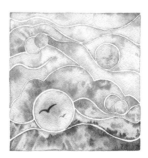

people coming together in harmony are a sign that the spirit of the Earth is there with you in your dreams, so use the opportunity to ask for a blessing of abundance or physical healing.

Wind/Sky: Cloudy skies and fog indicate obstacles or difficulties with people or troubles. Clear skies, on the other hand, mean that the path ahead is clear and open.

A NEW LANGUAGE

Much like learning a new language, this is a code to familiarise yourself with. According to the Aztec tradition, the dream state produces four times more energy than the waking, which is why our dreams so powerfully determine our waking lives. It takes a huge amount of discipline to become a master of dreams: to become regularly lucid, to "plant" successfully, find those dreams and watch them manifest in our waking lives, as well as to resist the compulsively habitual pattern to go down into those underworlds time and time again.

However, don't despair! This all takes time and practice. There is a simple technique to destroy dreams with negative and troubling influences – at least the ones we can remember. You can analyse your dreams according to the list above to decide if a dream is desirable to your life or not.

DREAM CANCELLATION WITH XIUHCOATL, THE FIRE SERPENT

Xiuhcoatl, the fire serpent, is often depicted in Aztec sculptures moving downwards with a pointy tail facing up. That's exactly what it'll be doing here.

* Imagine a picture of the dream you want to cancel and hold it in your forehead.

* Put fire there and watch it begin to burn.

* Visualise the fire forming a serpent's head facing downwards.

* This fire serpent is travelling down your whole body burning through any energetic imprint of the dream.

* Once it reaches your feet, stamp twice with one foot (either side) and ask the Earth to accept this dream.

* Stamp twice again and ask the Earth to turn it into something beautiful.

* Feel the serpent and the energy of the dream exiting from your foot into the Earth.

* Give thanks.

Xiuhcoatl

CHAPTER 4

The Aztec calendar and astrology cycle

The image of the Aztec calendar is one of the famous features of the culture, and was central to the Aztecs' way of life. The calendar consists of a 360-day civil cycle, called *xiuhpōhualli*, plus five days of darkness, the *nemontemi*. Then there is the 260-day ritual cycle, called the *tonalpohualli*.

Two of the most relevant features of Aztec astrology are in the system's 20 glyphs: each day in the calendar is assigned one of these glyphs, and there are also 20 solar waves or *trecenas* – 13-day periods – within the 260-day ritual cycle. Each glyph also rules one of these 13-day cycles and has a direction which is beneficial to ritual meditation and work, and they determine a soul's purpose and, potentially, a life's work. So, you have a day glyph sign with a number and your solar wave sign. As an example, my day glyph is 12 Cozcacuauhtli with Coatl solar wave. These will be listed below.

Each *trecena* is allocated for the way in which it can work spiritually and ritualistically with the energies of its particular glyph. For instance, *Cipactli*, a sea monster who is part crocodile, part fish and part frog (see opposite), is ideal for increasing abundance.

When an Aztec child was born, their astrological chart was calculated, which helped to make decisions on how the life path and education of each individual was decided. The Aztecs even had specific temples for each profession: someone born within the *Cuetzpalin* (Lizard) *trecena*, for example, would be sent to the appropriate school and temple when they were at the right age, in order to train in cultivating and working with the sexual energy and sex practices of the *Cuetzpalin*.

The 20 glyphs of Aztec astrology

These are the 20 glyphs of Aztec astrology and the significance of their *trecena* placements.

CIPACTLI (CROCODILE)

This sign has a strong connection with the Earth. People born under *Cipactli* are stable, slow and focused on security, money and the material world. Sometimes they can end up caring for family members and others, as they have a strong sense of responsibility which can often mean they become providers.

Trecena: Farmer, commerce, finance. Any profession connected to the Earth.

Cardinal point: East

EHECATL (WIND)

Like the wind itself, people born under *Ehecatl* tend to change a lot, both within themselves and in their lives. They sow seeds for the future, are intelligent and have the potential to do powerful work. *Ehecatl* is also the glyph of music, song and words. The wind carries the prayer; the clear sky is the dream of the wind. The day assigned to *Ehecatl* is also the day to work with the four winds. **South:** this blue wind removes thorns from your path. It brings willpower and wisdom. **North:** the black wind brings tragedy. **East:** the yellow wind brings blessings. **West:** the red wind purifies.

Trecena: Politicians, speakers, writers, poets and singers.

Cardinal point: North

CALLI (HOUSE, TEMPLE)

Though people born under *Calli* are structured, spiritual and reliable, and provide love and inner knowledge, they are also shy and do not always find relationships easy, as they can hide their feelings. *Calli* is connected to the home and the idea of a haven,

Trecena: Priests/priestesses, mystics, shamans and home-makers.

Cardinal point: West

CUETZPALIN (LIZARD)

Lizards are highly sexed and very fertile creatures, which means that *Cuetzpalin* is the glyph of sexual and creative energy. Sometimes this means that those born under it can have lots of children. They also have a need to be liked and to receive a lot of attention, and can be vain with their appearance. *Cuetzpalin* is also about ancestral knowledge, magical energy and the power of hypnosis, making it is easy for those assigned to it to manifest what they want, or to attract an audience and/or followers.

Trecena: Commercial matters, geishas, sex workers and performers.

Cardinal point: South

COATL (SERPENT)

These people are good healers, have wisdom and a very strong energy. However, because of this, they can sometimes find it difficult to relate to people whose energy is in a different frequency, potentially leading to problems with relationships, which can lead to isolation. It's difficult for them to relate to others on a different frequency. They can also be vengeful. As it represents all types of energy, the *Coatl* glyph is particularly suited for training in *nahualism*, as those who are born under it are always looking for renewal and change – just like the serpent, or snake, they are constantly seeking to shed their skin. There is a connection here to Kundalini energy in yoga, which is the energy that travels up the spine.

In the Aztec tradition, snakes are lucky and, as with many other traditions, linked to medicine and physical healing. As such, those studying medicine were advised to go to the mountains in order to find a snake to help them establish knowledge.

Trecena: Doctors, medicine, healers and *nahualism* (especially women).

Cardinal point: East

MIQUITZLI (DEATH)

Death invites major change into the lives of the people born under this glyph – and often not through choice. These people also look for wisdom, and there is great potential for healing, transformation and transmutation, which makes *Miquitzli* a potent glyph for *nahualism*.

Trecena: Death doula, funeral directors and undertakers.
Cardinal point: North

MAZATL (DEER)

Mazatl people have very strong perceptive powers and are prophetic. Like wild deer, they are very sensitive to vibrations, they seek freedom and love to be in the wild. Though sometimes pleasure-seeking and hedonistic, they can also be fearful, which can lead to them running away when afraid. In relationships, however, they have a strong sense of loyalty.

Trecena: Prophets, good at divination or psychic readings, running sweat-lodge ceremonies and dancers.
Cardinal point: West

TOCHTLI (RABBIT)

Tochtli is all about fecundity, and people born under this glyph find it easy to make things grow. They are intelligent and creative but also have a reputation for being addictive. Having favour with the moon, however, they can ask it for help. Such a connection also gives them great potential with dreamwork.

Tochtli has a link with *pulque*, an alcoholic drink in Mexico which is made from the maguey cactus.

Trecena: Alcohol production, any work involving moon rituals, surrogate mothers, creative and intellectual fields.

Cardinal point: South

ATL (WATER)

Much like water, people born under *Atl* have a strong sense of direction and purpose, and adapt to their surroundings. Emotions and relationships are key to them, and their use of words can harm as easily as it can heal. Their day number (see page 83) will determine what that relationship is, and the primary lesson they take from it.

There are four types of water that you can work with. Water days are good for working to balance your relationship to your own water and emotions: **Drought**: closed to emotions; **Flood**: intense emotions, prone to overreaction; **Hail**: addictions and destructive emotions; **Rain**: makes things grow and flourish, promises a great life.

Trecena: Fishermen, agriculture, marine biologist, diving instructor, sailor. Communication with water spirits, rivers and so on.
Cardinal point: East

ITZCUINTLI (DOG)

Itzcuintli has a strong link to the ancestors and ancestral patterns. People born under this glyph have the potential to free themselves from the patterns of their bloodline, or can just as easily repeat them.

Like dogs, they are loyal and friendly, and are travellers who like to explore. Change is a constant for them as they always want to change things. *Itzcuintli* is also about transmuting duality and is a good sign for training in *nahualism*.
Trecena: Tax collectors, accountants, bureaucracy and mediums. With their link to the land of the dead, people born under *Itzcuintli* can assist people in crossing over. In Aztec times, they were chosen as rulers.
Cardinal point: North

OZOMATLI (MONKEY)

This is the glyph of all the creative arts, and, just like monkeys, people born under *Ozomatli* are fun and joyful. When out of balance, however, they can be unreliable and irresponsible, with a tendency towards hedonism. The monkey is also the child of flowers, which gives this glyph a connection to plants.

Trecena: Dancers, performers, artists, writers, musicians and designers.
Cardinal point: West

MALLINALLI (IVY)

Mallinalli has a very strong connection to the plant world and what shamanic traditions would call "power" or "teacher" plants, such as peyote, ayahuasca, cannabis and psilocybin (magic mushrooms). People born under this glyph can train as healers, particularly with plants.

Like the ivy, these people have tenacity, but they can also twist and turn, which does not always make them predictable or easy to understand. When out of balance they can be manipulative. They can also be trapped in delusion, not wanting to face reality, and sometimes escape it with drugs and alcohol.

An important lesson of the *Mallinalli* glyph is to learn how to forgive, as people born under this sign can be judgemental, self-critical, and feel the need to improve things. Another aspect they may have to face is that of betrayal, which can also become a big theme in these peoples' lives.

Mallinalli can have the gift of balancing discipline and practicality with working with magic and the unseen.
Trecena: Plant shamans, herbalists, healers, *nahualism*.
Cardinal point: South

ACATL (REED)

Acatl is the arrow of knowledge and the glyph of leaders. It is the hollow reed, like bamboo, which the divine use as the conduit to teach those born under *Acatl* how to lead people. These people are intelligent and powerful, and can be ruthless and heartless; sometimes, when leading, they can get swept up in too much emotion, which clouds clear decision-making. However, when they are evolved, through self-reflection, and have attained the essence of their inner self, they will ultimately lead for the greater good and with loving intentions, rather than for personal gain or to dominate others.

Trecena: Leaders.

Cardinal point: East

OCELOTL (JAGUAR)

People born under *Ocelotl* can often be faced with many problems in life. The glyph is also known as "Sun of the Underworld" – the underworld is the jaguar's realm, where all a person's problems and shadowy aspects are brought into sharp focus. They have

the potential to face and overcome these issues, or stay stuck and be addicted to drama. If they succeed in overcoming them, they can become very powerful and lead or teach others to overcome their own personal underworlds. This gives them the potential to reach large numbers of people.

The jaguar is a warrior glyph and the Aztecs had jaguar warriors that were a group of military elite. This means that those born under *Ocelotl* are tenacious, cautious and have dignity and beauty. They also possess a strong connection to the night, and the potential to train in *nahualism*.

Trecena: Warriors, *nahualism*, psychologist and volunteers. They can help people overcome their underworlds.

Cardinal point: North.

CUAHTLI (EAGLE)

Cuahtli is the glyph of leadership, power and spiritual flight. It is the *nahual* of the sun. Suited to *nahualism*, this is the most powerful sign for lucid dreaming, though people born under Cuahtli can also be arrogant. Like eagles, they love to soar, and they tend to aim high in life, possessing a spiritual vision that gives them courage and tenacity.

As with jaguars, the Aztecs had eagle warriors who were also a group of military elite.

Trecena: Leaders, warriors, dreamers and *nahualism*.

Cardinal point: East

COZCACUAUHTLI (NECKLACE EAGLE OR VULTURE)

These people attract into their lives situations and people with heavy energy. Like the vulture, which can consume dead creatures and gain sustenance from them, while other animals would be poisoned, those born under *Cozcacuauhtli* can survive intense circumstances. Their lesson is to gain wisdom from this and find balance, so they can stop attracting this heaviness. As such, they can become the wisest people, and others will look to them for wisdom. Though in constant movement, they have patience and intuition, along with longevity and youthfulness.

Trecena: Advisors, psychologists, witches and wizards. They can take out bad energy and guide others along their paths.

Cardinal point: South.

OLLIN (MOVEMENT)

Ollin is the *nahual* of Quetzalcoatl, the feathered serpent. People born under this glyph are very intelligent and profound: all about progression, they put things in motion and can be revolutionary. Constantly active and always in motion, and with so much change going on around them, the challenge

that *Ollin* people face is to find stability in their lives.

Trecena: Supervisor, travelling jobs, innovators and motivational roles. Also dance and fitness roles.

Cardinal point: East

TECPATL (KNIFE OF JUSTICE)

Justice and fairness are important to people born under *Tecpatl*. They are very articulate and intelligent, but though they have a clear vision they can be blunt, which means sustaining relationships can be difficult. Their search for knowledge never ends.

Trecena: Judges, dreamers, writers, speakers and seekers of truth, they seek to re-establish justice in both waking and dream states.

Cardinal point: North.

QUIAHUITL (RAIN)

The *Quiahuitl* glyph can have a very destructive or constructive influence, depending on the day number it is combined with. Their challenge is to find balance within this flow of emotion – think of hail causing destruction, a lack of rain causing drought, or the welcome rain nourishing the plants and crops which feed us. These people have a lot of imagination and can be generous, but they can also be ambivalent, changeable, emotional, calm, peaceful or – when in extreme situations – violent.

Trecena: Psychologists, weather shamans, diplomats and ambassadors who are good at purifying situations.

Cardinal point: West

XOCHITL (FLOWER)

Xochitl is the most auspicious of the 20 glyphs. There are many possibilities with it, as it includes the qualities of all the other glyphs. Flowers have the high potential to achieve enlightenment, such as the blooming lotus flower on the crown of the head, which represents open spiritual channels and an evolved consciousness.

Embodying beauty, creativity and sensitivity, people born under *Xochitl* often have many interesting projects and a clear direction. They have many positives, but these positives can flip into negative dualities when they are not balanced.

These people have the potential to flower and not come back – i.e. to become enlightened.

Trecena: All of the other glyphs' trecena listings.

Cardinal point: South.

The 13 trecena day numbers

Each *trecena* consists of 13 days, numbered from one to 13. These numbers have particular qualities and are combined with the glyphs in order to gain a deeper understanding of the person born on that day. This might reveal important life lessons that person will learn, or how they can work with the energies of that day in a spiritual or practical way.

CE (ONE)
Indicates leaders or initiators of projects, but also people who have problems finishing or keeping up with projects.

OME (TWO)
Ome offers balance and grants structures to ideas. Because it is dualistic, it can be extreme.

YEI (THREE)
Yei is sacred number, and the number of fire. Adding character and strength, it relates closely to structure, the home and the fireplace. It is also the number of blood, which connects us to our ancestors and can take on the quality of violence. People born under *Yei* can learn lessons from repeating ancestral patterns; they may show an attachment to family, or the opposite.

NAHUI (FOUR)

The number of order, structure and equilibrium, *Nahui* is considered a good number, as all four of the elements are present. A lot of Aztec spiritual practices are carried out in four rounds because this is considered to be complete and harmonious. Think of the four seasons, or the four phases of the moon.

MAHCUILLI (FIVE)

Mahcuilli is the number of perfection and of spiritual connection. People born under this number have the potential to become whatever they want with this number. However, it comes with the challenge to not waste that potential. This number also means "to grab" – five being the number of fingers we have on each hand.

CHICOACEN (SIX)

Chicoacen represents the power of the serpents unified, bringing to mind the caduceus – the staff of Hermes – and the Kundalini, or serpent, energy in the yogic traditions. It contains all possibilities, from being born a saint to being born a murderer.

CHICOME (SEVEN)

Connecting life and death, *Chicome* is the creative force for good or bad, and represents the "One" in the middle of two opposing forces. It is also representative of the spiral.

CHICUEY (EIGHT)

Chicuey represents hidden and forbidden things – the inner things that have the potential to be drawn out and fulfilled to their fullest.

CHICNAHUI (NINE)

Chicnahui is an important number, as it is the number of both the underworld and of heaven – of above and below. As such, it represents command of communication with all the forces. The challenge for those born under this number is that *Chicnahui* emphasises repetitive destructive patterns and ancestral problems from which they need to break free.

MAHTLACTLI (TEN)

Representing creativity, duality, manual ability and skill, *Mahtlactli* is where potential is developed. Think of two hands with ten fingers; it is both the mother and the father.

MAHTLACTLI ONCE (ELEVEN)

Coming after *Mahtlactli*, *Mahtlactli Once* – or 11 – is the start of a new cycle. The challenge for those born under it is to decide whether to rest here or to persevere. Another option is to constantly start anew, though this does not sustain anything.

Planning, visualising, expression, words and verbalising are all significant themes that come under the number 11.

MAHTLACTLI OMOME (TWELVE)

Mahtlactli Omome represents creativity and duality: it is clarity of direction after a rest (*Mahtlactli Once*). With lucidity and clear vision, those born under it will understand their ancestral lineage and origin. It is the number of joyfulness, luminosity and cordiality, allowing for a deep search for understanding, for the meaning of life and knowledge.

MAHTLACTLI ONYEI (THIRTEEN)

As the last number in the set, whoever is blessed with being born under *Mahtlactli Onyei* has the potential to achieve whatever they set their mind to. It is a flowering number which has the energy to make things blossom. As the number of the sun, of precious knowledge and luck, it also has great creative potency which should be developed by any person born under it.

Aztec Calendar months

ATLACAHUALO 12-31 MARCH

These people are prone to mood swings and changeable feeling. Good luck and abundance. It is recommended to work ritualistically with rain.

TLACAXIPEHUALIZTLI 1-20 APRIL

This month is all about the power of renewal. These people are leaders and powerful. Change and shedding. Earth rituals.

TOZOZTONTLI 21 APRIL-10 MAY

Mystics. Strong character. Willpower. Rain rituals.

HUEHYI TOZOZTLI 11-30 MAY

Power of creation. Night rituals.

TOXCATL 31 MAY-19 JUNE

Emotional duality but have the potential to develop strong willpower.

ETZALCUALIZTLI 20 JUNE-9 JULY

Powerful and lucky. Sun rituals.

TECUHILHUITONTLI 10-29 JULY

Powerful. Ambivalent. Aggressive. Warriors. Lakes, rivers and seas.

HUEY TECUHILHUITL 30 JULY- 18 AUGUST

Leadership. Arrogant. Willpower. Full moon rituals.

TLAXOCHIMACO 19 AUGUST-7 SEPTEMBER

Connection to the power of death, the ancestors and dreams.

XOCOTL HUETZI 8-27 SEPTEMBER

These people have a tendency towards repeating ancestral patterns for good or bad. Fire rituals. Working with fire spirits.

OCHPANIZTLI 28 SEPTEMBER-17 OCTOBER

Helping others. Clean and clear energies to open new paths. Healers. Working with the elements water, wind, earth and fire.

TEOTLEHCO 18 OCTOBER-6 NOVEMBER

Those born in this month have a lot of mystic power. This is the time of year when the energy of the Earth is stored in the ground. Earth rituals.

TEPEILHUITL 7-26 NOVEMBER

People born in this month help the collective. Working with mountains and caves.

QUECHOLLI 27 NOVEMBER-16 DECEMBER

These people are dreamers. They work with the Moon and the night.

PANQUETZALIZTLI 17 DECEMBER-5 JANUARY

Warriors. Rising Sun.

ATEMOZTLI 6-25 JANUARY

These people are the best workers as they have a lot of energy. Rain.

TITITL 26 JANUARY- 14 FEBRUARY

These people have less energy. They work well with the Obsidian mirror. Cold and snow.

IZCALLI 15 FEBRUARY- 6 MARCH

Renewal. Pioneers. Abilities to create new things. Fire/Sunrise/Winter Solstice.

Calculating astrological charts

The information needed in order to calculate your and other peoples' astrological charts go way beyond the scope of this book. For those who wish to explore this further, I have provided a resource for practitioners that do this, and for my teacher, who teaches how to calculate astrological charts (see page 159). Be aware that there are many free websites whose chart calculations differ.

CHAPTER 5

Traditional spiritual cleansings

There are many ways to cleanse your energy field and this is something that's still extremely popular today, as a trip to the Zócalo, the main square in the historic quarter of Mexico City, will show you. Traditional practitioners are there daily, offering *limpias* (Spanish for spiritual cleansings), with tourists and locals alike queuing up to receive them.

Copal

Copal is a tree resin, which is burned as incense. It most commonly comes from the torchwood family of trees and was sacred to the Aztecs, who considered it to be the embodiment of Quetzalcoatl in the form of a plant – burning it was seen to be a way of bringing in his presence. It cleanses negative energy, purifies spaces and kills bacteria with its antiseptic qualities. It clears the way for positive energy and can lift depression, offering a brighter outlook. It is also seen to offer protection from negative energy and outside influences.

Ideal for use prior to a ritual or prayer work, copal strongly enhances a sacred connection to the spirit world; the smoke sends our prayers to the gods. It was used in funerary rites to bless the body and also to assist the soul on its passage to the afterlife. Copal can be used anytime but when used at noon it adds the full power of the sun to your work. Copal comes in different types and colours, but my preference is to

Spiritual cleansings in the Zócalo in Mexico City

burn white copal, where possible. You can buy Mexican incense bowls for burning it, which resemble a ceramic chalice. These can be picked up and moved around easily, which reduces the risk of getting burned.

COPAL CLEANSING ON YOURSELF AND OTHERS

For this you will need a heatproof incense burner (you may need a cloth to put this on or to move it with, depending on how hot it gets), a charcoal disc, which you can buy from spiritual shops or online, matches or a lighter and copal resin. For moving the smoke, you can use

Copal burning in ceramic cup on Day of the Dead altar

a large feather, fan or your hand. Alternatively, if you want to simplify things you can buy copal incense sticks.

SMUDGING A SPACE

Prepare the copal in the same way as before and move around the space, going into corners. Progress around the walls and the entire room at least once in a circuit. Open the door or a window so that the copal can take the negative and stagnant energy out of the room.

Charcoal disc and copal resin

SMUDGING FOR YOURSELF

* For the resin you will need to light the charcoal disc. Be careful with it as it can spark up quite quickly. Place it in the heatproof bowl. Be mindful that this bowl can get very hot, so think about what you are putting it on – and don't touch it until long after it has cooled down.

* Wait until the disc is white hot. You can gently blow on it to speed up this process.

* Place a small lump of resin on the disc.

* Offer the smoke to the six directions, waving it up and down and in a cross.

* Start bathing yourself in smoke at the top of your head, working your way down, spending longer on anywhere that feels more "sticky" or heavy.

* Make sure you do your hands and the soles of your feet.

* Do the back of your body, to the best of your abilities, being careful not to drop the contents of the bowl.

* Pay particular attention to the back of the knees and inside your elbows.

* Give thanks.

SMUDGING FOR OTHERS

* For the resin you will need to light the charcoal disc. Be careful with it as it can spark up quite quickly. Place it in the heatproof bowl. Be mindful that this bowl can get very hot, so think about what you are putting it on – and don't touch it until long after it has cooled down.

* Wait until the disc is white hot. You can gently blow on it to speed up this process.

* Place a small lump of resin on the disc.

* Offer the smoke to the six directions, waving it up and down and in a cross.

* Ask the person to open their arms sideways so they are shaped like a cross.

* Start at the top of their head, thoroughly working your way down the body, getting into any "corners" again, such as the knees and the elbows.

* Smudge the arms and the palms too.

* When you are at the feet, ask the person to lift up one foot at a time and smudge the bottom of each foot.

* Draw a cross down the central channel of the body and horizontally across the arms.

* Draw a circle around the person, sealing in the aura.

* Ask the person to turn around and do the same on the back of the body.

* Spend longer on any parts that feel sticky or dense.

* Give thanks.

Egg limpia

The Aztecs also performed egg *limpias*, or cleansings, but this is a practice that's used all over the world. The egg is considered to have the capacity to absorb huge amounts of negative energy from a person – and they give out positive energy in return. Advanced practitioners can crack open an egg and read the patterns in and around it.

Egg cleansings can be used to free up problems in all areas of your life:

❖ When you seem consistently to have "bad luck".

❖ When your mind is not clear and you are forgetful, or finding it hard to concentrate.

❖ For conflicts – or distance – in relationships.

❖ To help with difficulties in manifesting – whether that's money, work, or a relationship and so on.

❖ For health issues, though please note it's not a replacement for professional medical assistance.

❖ To clear negativity directed towards you, such as anger and jealousy.

❖ For stagnancy in your life or when you feel as if your path is blocked.

Egg *limpias* are a fantastic practice for enhancing your sense of well-being and attracting good things to you. You can use the method below to perform one for yourself or for others – even for your pets. Before you start, you will need an egg, which should be as fresh as possible, a glass for water and salt.

HOW TO PERFORM AN EGG CLEANSING

* Mix the salt with some water in the glass, leaving enough room to crack the egg in it after the cleansing. The salt stops the negative energy from coming out of the egg.

* Take the egg in your dominant hand. Say a prayer to set the intention:

* "I call on you, Divine Spirit, to bless this egg and remove all impurities from [enter name]. *Ometeotl*."

* Start at the head, rubbing the person with the egg in small circles.

* Go down the whole body, covering every inch.

* Use your intuition. If any areas feel like they need more work, stay with them until you sense it's right to move on.

* Visualise the egg absorbing everything that it needs to.

* Make sure you do the soles of your feet.

* When you are finished, crack the egg into the glass of salty water. Throw away the shell immediately, outside of the place that you are in.

* Check to see if there are bubbles – these generally represent jealousy captured in the egg by your ancestors. Cloudiness represents bad energy that has been removed.

* Don't leave the egg out for more than 45 minutes. Flush it down the toilet with the salt water.

* Clean the glass thoroughly to make sure all traces of the egg are gone.

The exercises above are simple, yet extremely powerful, practices for self-care and maintenance of your wellbeing. The Aztecs placed great importance on spiritual hygiene. In the next chapter, we will look at the consciousness of minerals.

CHAPTER 6

The consciousness of minerals

In the Aztec tradition, minerals were considered to possess a higher level of consciousness than humans. Though they appear static to us in our waking state, in the dream state they are more powerful and evolved. The Aztecs had many uses for them: spiritual, practical and aesthetic. Here are some of the most important.

Obsidian

Of huge significance for the Aztecs – and, indeed, across the Mexican traditions – obsidian demands due reverence. (The Nahuatl word for obsidian is *Itzli*, the name for the god of stone. Itzli is also an aspect of Tezcatlipoca, the Nahuatl for which, as we saw in Chapter 2, is "smoking mirror".) A powerful, sacred and practical tool for the Aztecs, obsidian is a mostly black volcanic glass, formed from fast-cooling lava. Used as a flint, or fashioned into extremely sharp blades and knives, many original obsidian tools now reside in museums. The stone is also believed to have magical, and healing properties.

There are different varieties of obsidian, such as silver or gold sheen, rainbow, blue, mahogany and "Apache tears" (black with white specks). Mahogany obsidian takes on a different quality and has associations with Xipe Totec, the god of spring and regeneration and the Red Tez-catlipoca (see Chapter 2). Obsidian is, however, all about the black: the void, and the land of the dead and the dreaming. It is one of the best

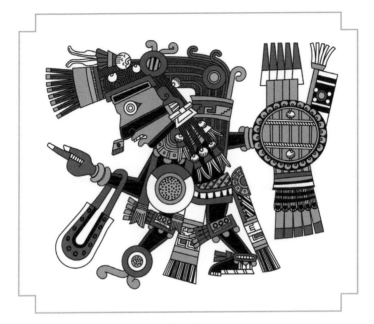

Tezcatlipoca

stones for bringing the unconscious into the conscious realm, and thus revealing truth.

TEZCATLIPOCA, RULER OF OBSIDIAN

Obsidian is ruled by the Aztec night deity Tezcatlipoca, associated with the colour black, and the black sun, the molten Earth's core from which obsidian is formed. Aztecs believed that when a volcano erupted, Tezcatlipoca was speaking.

As the essence of the light and the dark – of duality – he is said to "be the one that gives everything and takes everything", or who "takes you to war or peace". There is a strong undercurrent of karma and justice here, though the Christians that sought to bring their religion to Central America destroyed most depictions of Tezcatlipoca.

CARING FOR OBSIDIAN

Obsidian is the remover of darkness, revealing what is hidden, unseen in the shadows. It was thought to create a protective field against negative energies, and also believed to have the ability to trap souls, especially in its reflective mirror surface.

The stone is a powerful absorber of energies, and it can cut through negative energies like arrows, which means it can also drain people of their own energy if they are excessively exposed to it. As such, obsidian must be used sparingly, and is best used in conditions where there is an excess of energy. Like all black stones, it is very grounding.

When not being used, obsidian should be kept in red silk, or at least in a red cloth. This will prevent users from unnecessarily taking on negative energies from those absorbed by the stone.

CLEANSING OBSIDIAN

✤ Place the obsidian object in your right hand (unless it is too big to hold).

❖ Use your left hand to draw four anti-clockwise circles around the object. This clears the energies from the stone.

❖ Draw a cross through the object. This prevents energies from going into or out of the obsidian – particularly if it is a mirror.

This same technique can be used to cleanse metal objects, such as jewellery or cutlery, and it is great for cleansing a home of unwanted energies.

OBSIDIAN, OR "SMOKING MIRROR"

Not only could obsidian be crafted into sharp blades, but it could also be polished into a perfectly smooth, reflective surface. Several obsidian mirrors are on display in the British Museum, in London, in particular the mirror once owned by the 16th-century astrologer John Dee, which he claimed belonged to Moctezuma himself. Recent research has confirmed that that his mirror was from Pachuca, where a lot of obsidian mining took place.

The obsidian mirror is also known as "smoking mirror", as it is common for people gazing into the mirror to see smoke or cloudlike images forming in its reflective surface. These were used for scrying, divination and healing; rulers used mirrors to observe their subjects and to see into the future.

Use of the mirror takes extensive training, involving many different eye positions with various purposes. One of these is known as cleansing the underworlds – a deep healing process.

Its use also ties into the Toltec creation myth of the original force of creation: the Black Eagle seeing its reflection, covered in Chapter 2. The belief is that our reflection in the mirror encompasses our perception of ourselves, our lives and the lives of those around us, and everything that happens to us – that the many filters we view life through are in

Aztec Black Eagle

fact just a reflection. When we learn to detach ourselves from what we perceive to be our reality and our problems, we can free ourselves from this social, familial and religious conditioning – what we have taken on from our ancestors and our past life experiences.

One aspect of working with the mirror is to enable ourselves to do this: to see all these things in the mirror and to ask the mirror to remove these energies from us, so we may return to the state of the Black Eagle and the void. This is true freedom. Training with the mirror is a big undertaking, but there are some starting points below.

WORKING WITH THE MIRROR

The obsidian mirror is a portal that sends out and takes in energy. As such, psychic hygiene is very important when working with the mirror.

THE BLACK EAGLE'S PERCEPTION

This is one of the many eye positions whose purposes vary (all of them are named after different birds). Practising this can give you an idea of how using the mirror can change your perception of things.

* Cleanse the mirror and put it in your lap.

* Perform four sets of nine breaths: inhalations through the nose, exhalations through the mouth. (The four rounds reflect the complete harmonious cycle, and the nine breaths put you in tune with the Black Tezcatlipoca.) Make them strong and quick. This puts you into an altered state of consciousness.

* Look into your reflection in the mirror.

* Move your eyes outwards to your peripheral vision. This may feel unnatural at first, as you are pushing your eyes out sideways, like a bird's, but you can train your eye muscles. Widen your focus outside the mirror.

* Slightly close your eyes, so that you are squinting. Do this until you see your face disappear in the mirror.

* If you have a particular issue or problem in mind, imagine that you are watching it disappear into the void.

* When you have finished, let your eyes rest in their usual position so that you can see your reflection.

* Place the mirror between your hands. Thank it and say "*Ometeotl*". This seals any shifts in energy that have occurred.

* Clean the mirror before you store it away.

* This is a powerful meditation. Try building up your abilities so that you can hold this gaze for longer and longer.

Every time you use your mirror, cleanse it before and afterwards, using the method detailed above.

THE EYE OF TEZCATLIPOCA

While performing the Black Eagle's perception, you may see a single eye looking back at you from the centre of the mirror. This is not your reflection. It is the eye of Tezcatlipoca.

As Tezcatlipoca is the one who gives everything, as well as takes everything away, you can ask the eye to see you how you would like to be seen, such as happy, completely healthy, or with a new job that you want. Conversely, you can ask the eye to see you without something you wish you did not have, like a sickness.

Jade

Along with quetzal feathers, jade was one of the most precious substances in the Aztec empire. Reserved purely for the use of priests and nobility, it was held in high spiritual reverence, and Aztec law made it illegal for anyone of a lower-class status to possess it. (The Nahuatl word for jade is *chalchihuitl*, which means "precious" and "heart of the Earth" – the Aztec equivalent to the expression "heart of gold" is "heart of jade".) Associated with maize, fertility, water and blood, jade was seen as having strong healing and medicinal properties, and was

used to cure internal ailments. Thought of as a kidney, spleen and liver healer, it was treated as a stone of longevity and rejuvenation that maintained youth. It was also believed to be a liquid that could make repairs and renew life.

Jade was also used extensively on people of nobility after death. If a piece of jade was placed on the deceased's lips close to the time of death, it was believed that the essence of the person would be captured in the stone. This is why small pieces of jade were placed in the mouths of corpses (sometimes they used emerald). After cremation, the stone was placed on the temple altar or in a special room in the royal palace. Jade was also considered to be able to connect with a higher power.

When important rulers died, their death masks were made of jade so that the lords of the underworld would recognise them and treat them with reverence.

Believed to be a dreaming stone, it was said that those who slept with jade could achieve states of lucid dreaming more easily.

JADE AS A CONNECTOR TO TLALOCAN, THE "PLACE OF PARADISE"

There is a fundamental link between jade and Tlaloc – "he who makes things sprout" – and Chalchiuhtlicue, "Lady of the Jade skirt" and the Aztec goddess of water. Tlaloc and Chalchiuhtlicue ruled over bodies of water and the rain.

Tlalocan was "the place of paradise": a heavenly realm for those who had died water-related deaths. More than that, it was considered a state of being that the living can aspire to – the bliss state, a state of happiness. (As explained in Chapter 2 about energy centres, jade has its own chakra on the forehead, the centre of our emotions.)

The Aztecs believed that jade could help us reach the place of paradise in our own earthly existence – to achieve balance and be in paradise within our own internal waters.

There are four states of water, as referenced in Chapter 4, under the glyph *Atl*. These can be linked to emotions or anything in our lives.

Drought: An emotional drought could be depression: a lack of joy. Or it could be a lack of compassion. If you are sick, it could be a lack

Tlaloc and Chalchiuhtlicue

of health. If you have very little money, it could be a lack of prosperity or abundance.

Flood: This is anything in excess, such as being quick to anger or constantly crying. Drinking and eating too much are physical ailments. Being a workaholic, over-thinking things, worrying a lot or being involved in conflict are other situations associated with the flood state.

Hail: These are destructive emotions or influences, such as receiving or speaking harsh words. Illnesses, arguments, accidents, disruptions and unhappy memories are also destructive.

Rain: The rain state offers the perfect balance and conditions for situations to flourish in harmony, leading to perfect health, happy relationships and stable emotions.

JOURNEY TO THE PLACE OF PARADISE

This exercise is for contemplating, healing and balancing your emotions. Reflecting on the state of the waters in your life enables you to come closer to a consistent place of happiness. Allow the precious essence of jade to take you there.

If you have a piece of jade – or, as jade has become increasingly rare, you can use nephrite, a type of jade – hold it, or place it on or near you during the meditation in order to utilise its healing effects. You can also place it in a glass of water, removing the jade before drinking the water at the end of the meditation.

* Sit in a comfortable position and close your eyes. Take a deep breath in and, as you exhale, feel that you have landed fully into your body.

* Take another deep breath and focus on connecting with the precious essence of jade.

* Take another deep breath and focus on journeying to the place of paradise. (After the exercise has finished, try to retain this connection in your everyday life.)

* Perform a round of ten inhalations through the nose, exhaling through the mouth. Ten is the number of the precious essence.

* Think about the droughts in your life – emotional or otherwise – and try to recall as many of these as possible.

* Feel the essence of jade removing these droughts from you, so that they can be rebalanced.

* Perform another round of ten breaths, in preparation for the next water.

* Now contemplate the floods in your life – anything that you have an excess of. These floods are creating the droughts.

* Feel the essence of jade absorbing the excess water from the issues, so that they drain away.

* Perform another round of ten breaths, in preparation for the third water.

* Reflect on where there is – or has been – hail in your life. These are any destructive emotions, situations and memories you hold on to. Start with key events, such as sicknesses, and continue through to anything that comes to mind that has brought you suffering.

* Feel the essence of jade absorbing and removing this hail and softening and rebalancing the waters of your internal universe.

* Perform another round of ten breaths, in preparation for the final water.

* Now see the rain falling on you in the perfect measure needed to bring nourishment and flowering to your life. See the plants and flowers, the projects and things you want to see bloom in your life, opening and flourishing in magnificence and beauty. Feel your internal universe come into a place of peace, balance and happiness.

* Then find yourself walking up a path made of shells. Follow this path until you reach the entrance of the Jade Garden, guarded by the Lord and Lady of the Waters (Tlaloc and Chalchiuhtlicue).

* Ask them to allow you to enter the garden. They will open the way for you, like a gate.

* Find yourself in a paradise full of waterfalls and gorgeous pools of water... A place to play and have fun. It is inhabited by butterflies, hummingbirds, monkeys and flowers beyond your wildest imagination.

* As you walk through this exquisite place, you notice the ground is covered everywhere with pieces of jade.

* Ask to find your piece of jade, and keep searching until you find it. You will know when it is in front of you.

* When you find your piece of jade, pick it up and hold it next to your heart.

* Feel the jade empowering you – healing your heart and emotions, and bringing your waters into harmony. Take the time to really allow this to happen.

* When you are ready, prepare yourself to return. Make a promise to retain the place of paradise inside yourself as much as you can. You are bringing all of this back with you.

* Count down from four to one.

* Come back. Feel yourself in your body.

Turquoise

The Nahuatl word for turquoise is *Xihuitl*, which has several meanings: year, comet and herb. Like jade, turquoise was considered extremely valuable – possibly even more valuable than jade – and was reserved only for those of the highest status, such as the emperor. Unlike most stones, its properties allow it to be melted into different forms.

Turquoise is closely associated with the god of war, Huitzilopochtli, and the souls of warriors. Used in shields and ceremonial masks, it was believed to offer protection against both physical enemies and negative spiritual forces.

Huitzilopochtli

It is also a sky stone. The Aztecs had Xiuhtecuhtli, "the Turquoise Lord", a fire deity/ essence, and his *nahual* spirit Xiuhcoatl, "the Turquoise Fire Serpent of meteoric fire", whom we met in the Chapter 3 – hence the link with comets and shooting stars. The Turquoise Fire Serpent has a distinctly segmented body, which links to the Aztecs' belief that, after comets strike the Earth, they then change into worms and caterpillars. Turquoise was also seen as a type of "star excrement".

As such, there is an essential link between turquoise and the element of fire – which may initially seem strange, given that its colour is such a strong blue – but when you look closely at a flame, the deep inner heart of its core is also blue.

Xiuhcoatl also means "young fire". It is a fire that can destroy things that we want to purify or be rid of. It is also a fire of expansion, such as growing a business.

GOLD, SILVER AND AMBER

Gold, silver and amber were seen as valuable and precious metals. Only the emperor was able to give gold gifts, and most often did so when they wanted to keep the peace or reward valiant soldiers.

Teocuitlatl is the word for precious metals, but it also means "excrement of the gods". For the Aztecs, the existence of the gods' excrement on Earth was a testament of their presence. Silver was seen as the excrement of the moon, and gold was believed to have come from the sun.

Both gold and amber are associated with Quetzalcoatl, and amber was frequently burned as offerings to the gods. The Spanish conquistadors recounted how Moctezuma II had used an amber spoon to stir his chocolate.

CHAPTER 7

Death and its significance to the Aztecs

"Like a painting we will fade away. Like a flower we have to dry on the ground, like a quetzal, the zacuan, the tile, we will perish." - Aztec proverb

Death is a central theme in Mexican culture. Today the Day of the Dead celebrations are world-renowned, and visitors to Mexico will notice an openness and dark sense of humour around the topic of death. The roots of this attitude can be traced to the ancient Mesoamerican cultures: the Aztecs, Toltecs and their predecessors.

The Aztec land of the dead, known as Mictlan, was ruled by a couple, Mictlantecuhtli and Mictecacihuatl, Lord and Lady of the Underworld, who are both depicted as skeletal figures.

Today Santa Muerte – the Mexican folk saint of death – has a large number of dedicated followers. It is thought she originated from Mictecacihuatl, whose power and influence are still strong today.

Mictecacihuatl and Mictlantecuhtli

DYING TO YOUR OLD SELF

In the Aztec tradition, dying is not just about physical death. Many life-changing experiences are viewed as a type of death – for example, being born, puberty, falling in love, becoming pregnant, giving birth or becoming a parent, divorce and breaking up from a partner. In healing work, we also look at ways a problem, a sickness or a situation might be made to "die".

CONSCIOUS DEATH AND REINCARNATION

The Aztecs and the Toltecs had deep and intricate knowledge of, and training around, death. It is difficult to fathom for the modern, rational mind, but death and life, according to the Aztec tradition, are simply different states, so putting all our emphasis on being alive in the physical body negates and dismisses a huge part of our existence. They believed in reincarnation and that when we die, we return until we reach a state of full flowering – or enlightenment, as it is more commonly known in the Eastern traditions.

During this transition between life and death, they believed we often lose a lot of our energy, or power, because most people die unconsciously. This idea is central to the dream training, which isn't just for manifestation or to read omens about the future and present. According to the Aztec tradition, the land of the dead is the same place we go to when we dream, so training in the dream state also teaches us to be able to operate with consciousness when we die. If we die an unconscious death, we can lose a lot of energy and create more problems in our next incarnation, and if we're involved in spiritual training, more work needs to be done to retrieve that energy. Learning to remain conscious while you dream is big step in dream warrior training: you are learning to die a conscious death. The Aztecs believed dying a conscious death would erase your sins, which would be considered controversial today for many people, but their belief was: know how to dream, know how to die, know how to live.

Aztec warrior with death mask

In the traditions, people not only trained to die consciously, but they considered the options of how they might exit their body. They believed these would determine how they would reincarnate and if they would come back in a human body at all.

Different ways to die

If you could choose, how would you like to die?

According to the Aztecs, there were different ways to exit the body and those who were highly trained in the art of conscious dying could choose how they wanted to continue their existence. Your energetic body and soul would be able to consciously exit out from one of the following centres.

LIVER

This is how most people die – it's an unconscious death, in which you go to the underworlds and reincarnate.

CHEST

In this instance, Aztecs believed you would go to the sun and merge with it, so you completely lose your identity and ego and don't come back in any physical form.

FOREHEAD

Exiting from here means that you become a *pipitlin* or angelic being (see Chapter 3). *Pipitlins* serve all beings unconditionally – they don't discriminate, serving the murderer and the saint alike.

CROWN OF THE HEAD

This is the Nahual's death: it means you are free and independent to do what you want to do. You can take on physical form and leave it at will. You can come back as a human to do something extraordinary, perhaps returning as a spiritual leader or genius musician, or anyone who has far-reaching impact. It's your choice.

PREPARATION FOR DEATH

Nine months before death, the Aztecs believed your consciousness receives a message letting you know, even if you are healthy. You will dream about your ancestors – this is the first call, as your consciousness wants you to prepare with the "Dead Ones". The idea was that people who don't work with the ancestors will wither in spirit and have less power and energy.

The other thing they considered important was to free yourself from attachments. Everything you receive in life is lent to you: your body, your home, your possessions, your relationships. If you move to the afterlife thinking of attachments, such as your home, you can get trapped – think of the classic story of the haunted house! If you know you have a particularly strong attachment to something or someone, you have time to address this and get to the root cause of the issue in order to release it.

Even illnesses can be carried over and brought over into the next incarnation. It was said that you shouldn't touch a corpse for up to four hours of the person dying as their energy was thought to be still leaving the body and you – and they – could get affected by it.

Day of the Dead

Day of the Dead has its origins in the Aztec culture – and way further back. It originally took place over several weeks in the summer from late July to the middle of August, which is the ninth month in the Aztec calendar. The Aztecs celebrated the death of their ancestors during this festival, as well as honouring and appeasing the Lord and Lady of the Underworld with offerings. The idea behind this festival is that the dead should be celebrated rather than remembered with sorrow – this is a party for them!

After conquering Mexico, the Spanish Catholics encouraged the locals to shift their summer festival to All Souls' Day, as they knew they could not completely eradicate the Aztec traditions. Practitioners of the traditions still celebrate from 31 October to 2 November, correlating to the month of the western astrology sign Scorpio, which also has a close affinity with death.

Women wearing traditional sugar skull masks and costumes for Day of the Dead

San Andrés Mixquic is a village outside Mexico City, which was once the site of an Aztec temple. Today it's best known for its huge Day of the Dead celebrations, which are centred around the Catholic church and cemetery there. The celebrations start on the evening of 31 October and continue until 2 November – when the bells ring that night, it signals that all the souls are returning to the other side.

One of the best ways to work with our ancestors is to use this time when the veil between the living and the dead is lifted – to celebrate them, connect with them and give them offerings, which is why altars with flowers, food, incense are built.

WORKING WITH THE CONSCIOUSNESS OF SKULLS

The Aztecs would also have permanent altars featuring the skulls of their ancestors, which were called *tzompantlis*, as we have seen, which means skull racks. The Aztecs believed consciousness was recorded inside skulls – a less common belief in modern times, of course, though skulls are still significant in Day of the Dead celebrations. Sugar skulls are thought to represent the deceased person and plastic and crystal skulls are something you will see in the celebrations as well.

Crystal skulls held a magical significance to the Aztecs. There are some famous examples in museums around the world, though scientists and archaeologists are sceptical about their authenticity. This doesn't mean that they did not exist. The Aztecs thought of them as dream diaries, which hold and record information.

DAY OF THE DEAD PARTY OFFERING

* Make sure you have pictures of everyone you want to invite: ancestors and loved ones who have passed over. If you don't have a picture, then use a sugar, plastic or crystal skull. Write or stick their name on the skull.

* Consider whether any relatives had qualities or talents that you want to cultivate in yourself. If so, then I recommend using a sugar skull for those individuals as their energy will be available for you to consume afterwards.

* Prepare food and drink, bearing in mind anything you are aware of that the deceased particularly liked. Do the same with preparing flowers, decorations and music.

* Have a candle for each person to put in front of their photo or skull.

* Use flower petals leading up from your door to the altar, which they can follow, and light the way with candles.

* Treat it like a party for the living with your offerings and your behaviour, so make sure you are there for the duration!

* After the Day of the Dead celebrations are over, if you have made the intention to consume the consciousness of certain ancestors, now is the time to eat their sugar skulls.

* You can keep a permanent altar to your ancestors and make regular offerings.

Traditional Day of the Dead altar with sugar skulls and candles

The significance of dogs and the afterlife

What in your life do you want to bring death to?

What do you want to bring life to?

Dogs were considered to have a particular significance as guides for people who have recently died as they cross over to the underworld. This idea was not exclusive to the Aztecs: the Egyptians had Anubis, the jackal-headed deity associated with death, and the Greeks had Cerberus, the three-headed dog that guarded the underworld.

The Aztecs had their very own temple dog Xoloitzcuintli, whose name came from two words: *Xolotl*, the god of lightning and death, and *Itzcuintli*, meaning dog. According to Aztec mythology, this hairless breed was made by Xolotl from a sliver of the "Bone of Life" from which all humans are made. Humans were entrusted with the task of guarding this dog with their lives – in return, it would guide people through the perils of the underworld towards the evening star. The breed nearly became extinct when the Spanish landed and used to kill and eat them, but they had a resurgence in popularity in the mid-20th century. Frida Kahlo loved them and had many as pets, and they can still be seen in some of the sacred sites today.

A Xoloitzcuintli dog

WORKING WITH ITZCUINTLI AND MIQUITZLI

Itzcuintli, the dog, offers another way to work with ancestors and the land of the dead and we can begin by planting it in our dreams (see Chapter 3 on dreams and dream-planting). We can also work with the calendar on the days and trecenas of *Iztcuintli* for healing the bloodlines and working with the ancestors.

Miquitzli – or death – days and trecenas are important to work with too – think about what you what you want to bring death to in your life and don't be afraid to contemplate how you want to die and how you want to live.

CHAPTER 8

The sacred plants of the Aztecs

The Aztecs considered many plants to be sacred, with uses that went beyond food and drink for pleasure and physical sustenance. A sign of their status can be seen in the fact that it was not permitted to be in the presence of Aztec royalty without offerings of flowers, and that certain flowers were only permitted to be handled by people with royal blood.

Bust of Xochipilli among flowers

Much of our knowledge of the way the Aztecs used plants comes from the *Florentine Codex*, written by the Spanish Franciscan friar Bernardino de Sahagún in the 16th century. As with minerals, the Aztecs believed that plants possessed a higher state of consciousness than humans, especially in the dream state. The ancient people of Mexico were also known to perform rituals with "teacher plants" or hallucinogenic plants.

Creative in the arts and sciences, the Aztecs were no less inventive when it came to cultivating plants. They bred double-flowered varieties of certain flowers, while popcorn, and even *chicle* – a natural chewing gum – dates back to the Aztec Empire.

Xochipilli, the god of flowers, love, beauty, pleasure and sacred plants, is one of the most famous gods or essences to be associated with plant life. Below is a selection of different plants that held special significance to the Aztecs.

Maize

Though a staple crop, maize was viewed as sacred because it was brought to the people by Quetzalcoatl. It was also associated with other deities: Centeotl, Chicomecoatl and Xipe Totec. The Aztecs used maize in many different ways, and it was central to various celebrations and rituals in their lives.

Part of the Aztec creation myth was that humans were created from maize, cacao and other plants from the Mountain of Sustenance. One story of how humans came to possess maize is that the gods and goddesses in Tamoanchan (paradise) were looking at the newly created but weak beings and wondered, "What shall the humans eat? Everyone must look for food for them."

Quetzalcoatl saw a red ant shelling corn in the shadows of a mountain. In order to get a closer look, he transformed himself into a black ant. The red ant led the disguised god to the mountain and showed him where the maize grew. Carrying a kernel on his back, Quetzalcoatl took it to the gods and goddesses, who examined it and agreed that this was good for humans to eat, and that they should be taught to grow the crop so that it could be one of their main food sources. The gods chewed on the maize, creating a paste that was put on the lips of the humans – energised by the new food source, the humans began to stir and get stronger.

Quetzalcoatl transformed into Tolpiltzen, the reforming priest of Tula, who taught the people all about agriculture so they could grow maize and other crops in order to sustain themselves.

Corn kernels also have an association with the four winds and are used for divination.

The maguey cactus

This sacred plant was used for a variety of purposes, as its fibres and spikes were perfect for fashioning ropes, fabrics, construction materials and shoes.

The agave cactus is perhaps the best-known type of maguey, thanks in part to agave syrup, a type of honey-water which has become a fashionable alternative to sugar. Fermented, it is also used in the production of pulque, mescal and tequila.

Maguey is the plant of the goddess Mayahuel, who had 400 breasts to feed her 400 rabbit children (*Tochtli*, the rabbit glyph of the calendar, is linked with intoxication). Pulque, a milky alcoholic drink linked with *Tochtli*, is considered a sacred drink that brings people closer to the divine. During the reign of the Aztec Empire, pulque was reserved for exclusive use by priests and priestesses.

Mescal, whose name means "the one coming from the moon", is also considered sacred. This drink can be used for changing consciousness, and was the first substance of its type given to humans for this purpose. When used correctly, it joins the *tonal* and the *nahual* in order to open up our perceptual abilities. It is also said that two of the angelic *pilpitlin* beings entered into mescal so that happiness could be experienced by humans.

Using these sacred drinks is, however, only effective when used in measurements of no more than two units. Exceeding this amount can cause users to lose consciousness while dreaming, so that they forget their dreams. It was also believed that drinking more than two measurements would put users under the spell of the moon in a destructive way, making them behave in ways that they otherwise wouldn't. (You only need to visit a town centre on a weekend night in any alcohol-friendly culture to witness this!)

Cacao

Cacao was revered as being a link between heaven and Earth. The Aztecs believed that the cacao tree was a gift to humans from Quetzalcoatl, who had come down to Earth from an afternoon star while bearing the gift. As such, it was thought to have contained the wisdom and divinity of Quetzalcoatl, which could be imbued upon consumption. Cacao was also considered to be the blood and bones of the gods, creating a link between cacao – whose pods are shaped like human hearts – and the heart.

The Mayans are credited with bringing cacao to the Aztecs, and though the Aztecs did not produce it locally, they used it as a form of currency and made it a central feature of ceremonial acts: it was used at funerary rites; couples would drink a cup of cacao at marriage ceremonies; and cacao beans were exchanged to aid fertility. It was also given out at the birth of a child and at baptisms. During religious rituals, cacao was often mixed with psilocybin mushrooms, and it was commonly offered to the gods, with drops of blood, from bloodletting practices, placed on the nibs.

A mood enhancer, cacao also had medicinal purposes. Cacao flowers were used to treat fatigue, and different cacao-based concoctions were used to treat fever, shortness of breath and to stimulate the nervous system of people who were apathetic, exhausted and weak. Thought to improve digestion and stimulate the kidneys, cacao was also prescribed for anaemia, mental fatigue, poor breast-milk production, low sex drive, gout and kidney stones. Warriors used it as a nutrient to boost their stamina, and believed that, through Quetzalcoatl's presence, it gave them insight to assist them in their battles.

XOCOLATL

Moctezuma II was notorious for his voracious appetite for cacao, which he mainly consumed in the traditional Aztec bitter chocolate water. He was reputed to drink 50 cups a day, from golden goblets, before entering his harem, which also gave rise to cacao's reputation as an aphrodisiac. Thousands of pitchers of cacao were also prepared on a daily basis for the palace residents.

Xocolatl, or "bitter water", has given us the modern word "chocolate". Apart from its medicinal administrations, which could come from different parts of the plant, cacao was most commonly consumed in the form of the bitter liquid which the Aztecs served cold. Rather than adding milk, the Aztecs used water and various spices, such as cornmeal, vanilla, chilli and sometimes magnolia flower. Though they are not said to have used sweetening agents, it is possible that honey was also used. Some scholars have even suggested that the Aztecs made the first version of a cappuccino, as they frothed their chocolate drink by pouring the liquid from one container to another, letting it fall from human height. The froth was said to be the most important part of the drink – the higher the froth, the better the drink and the cook. Later, the Spanish introduced the *molinillo* (chocolate whisk) to the process, in order to create the froth. This recipe, based on accounts of the original *xocolatl* drink, will allow you to experience the Aztec drink for yourself.

Ingredients

- ✤ 2¾ cups water

- ✤ ⅛ cup unsweetened cocoa powder/raw cacao powder (If you are really dedicated, you can grind the equivalent in cacao nibs.)

- ✤ 1 green chilli, sliced

- ✤ 1-2 vanilla pods
  Scrape the contents
  from inside the
  pods.

- ✤ ½ tsp cinnamon
  powder

- ✤ Optional: allspice to
  taste

- ✤ Optional: honey to
  sweeten

Heart-shaped cacao pods

Method

+ Take ¾ of a cup of water and the green chilli, including the seeds, and add to a pan. Bring it to the boil and let it simmer for five to ten minutes, to really infuse the water with the chilli.

+ Strain off the chilli and put the water back into the pan.

+ Add the other 2 cups of water to the pan. Add the vanilla and put onto a medium heat until it comes to boil.

+ Add the cocoa. Whisk it as it simmers for another five minutes, then leave to cool

+ If you want to try the traditional frothing take an extra container and pour from one container to the other, with the receiving container on the floor. (If possible, do this outside, as some of the mixture will splash onto the floor.)

+ Serve in a golden goblet and sweeten with honey if desired!

+ Feel the wisdom of Quetzalcoatl coursing through your veins.

Vanilla

Tlilxochitl, meaning "black flower" in Nahuatl, originally came from the Totonac people, who were from Veracruz, on the Mexico coast. They were conquered by the Aztecs, who developed a fondness for the black flower and received it in tribute from the Totonacs.

The Totonacs had a dramatic legend for vanilla's origins, involving Princess Xanat, who fell in love with a mortal. Her father forbade such a relationship, so she fled with her lover to the forest, where they were captured and beheaded. It was said that when their blood touched the ground, the tropical flowers grew.

The Aztecs had several uses for vanilla. A perfume and an aphrodisiac, it also had a symbiotic relationship with cacao, as the two ingredients enhanced each other. It was also used as a remedy for indigestion, and a treatment for lice and fatigue.

Damiana

Renowned for being a powerful aphrodisiac, this herb was also seen as a tonic that could provide multiple health benefits for overall wellbeing.

Reputedly a mood-enhancer and antidepressant, damiana was famed for its use as an aid for the loss of libido in men and women, for its benefits for fertility and hormonal balance, and for alleviating premenstrual pains. It was also used to aid digestion and soothe the nervous system while increasing stamina and cleaning the lungs.

Like mescal, damiana was also used to enhance lucid dreaming abilities and increase vivid dreams. Try the tea recipe below, in order to see the effects for yourself. If you want it to affect your dreams, drink it just before sleeping.

- ❖ Take 1 tsp of dried damiana and put it in a cup or a teapot.
- ❖ Fill with boiling water and leave for 15 to 20 minutes, covered.
- ❖ Strain into another cup.
- ❖ Add honey to sweeten if desired.

Marigolds

In Nahuatl, *zempoalxochtli* means "20 flowers" or "flower of many petals", and marigolds are famously associated with Day of the Dead celebrations, in which they are still used to decorate graves, altars and ofrendas, or offerings, to the deceased. Their strong fragrance and vibrant colour are said to attract and guide the souls of the dead back to the land of the living during the festival.

Marigolds are also associated with the sun, while the Aztecs, whose horticultural skills enabled them to breed fantastically large flowers, believed that all flowers are linked with the fragility of life. Like vanilla, this special flower has a romantic myth attached to its origins. Xochitl and Huitzilin met as children and fell in love. Together, they loved to climb their favourite mountain and offer flowers to the sun god Tonatiuh, who shone his warm rays down upon them in appreciation. On that mountain, Xochitl and Huitzilin swore their eternal love and commitment to each other.

Huitzilin was subsequently sent to fight in a war, during which he was killed. Devastated by the news, Xochitl climbed the mountain and prayed to Tonatiuh that he might reunite her with her lover on Earth. Moved by her prayers, Tonatiuh shone his light upon her and, as the rays touched her cheek, she transformed into the radiant marigold flower, containing the essence of the sun itself. Huitzilin was then re-incarnated as a hummingbird, and he flew to touch the centre of the flower with his beak. Opening its many petals, the flower released its powerful scent. As long as marigolds and hummingbirds exist on the Earth the two lovers will always be together.

Marigold flowers are edible and were also used as a dye and for food colouring. The Aztecs believed them to have many medicinal properties, too, including alleviating stomach and respiratory ailments, combating parasites, soothing hiccups and to heal people who had been struck by lightning.

Tobacco

Named *picietl* – "little perfume" – in Nahuatl, the Aztecs' tobacco was a far cry from the weakened and chemically-loaded substance used to produce cigarettes today. Medicinally, it was used for enemas, wound dressings, toothache, diarrhoea, gout, fatigue and headaches. It was also a pesticide and applied to treat poisonous bites.

Tobacco contained pleasurable properties, too: there are accounts of people smoking tobacco from a reed pipe after enjoying a post-banquet cup of cocoa.

The goddess Chihuacoahuatl's body was said to be made out of tobacco, which gave it a huge spiritual and religious significance to the Aztecs. Tobacco was also seen as a gift from the gods, and the tobacco flower – along with *teonanacatl* (see opposite) – was often carved into the base of statues of Xochipilli.

Tobacco was drunk in infusions, smoked and chewed in order to produce altered states of conscious-

Xochipilli statue - base carved with tobacco flower and teonanacatl ness, and used as offerings, often in the form of smoke rising to the heavens. Some Aztec healers specialised in working with tobacco as an aid to enable more insight into their client's condition, and to divine what was needed to help. Skilled in reading the smoke and the shapes in the ash on the head of cigars, they would blow smoke on and around a client's body, reading the smoke in order to see where there were blockages. Much like copal smoke, tobacco smoke was also believed to be able to assist in clearing these blocks. Tobacco was also seen as a powerful protector against evil spirits.

Teonanacatl

Believed to be the flesh of the gods – another gift from Quetzalcoatl – *teonanacatl* were hallucinogenic psilocybin mushrooms eaten in sacred ceremonies, often after drinking the bitter *xocolatl* drink, and sometimes in a wine-like infusion with pulque. The Aztecs believed the mushrooms induced a powerful visionary state in which prophetic revelations could be received. As with all of these plants, they were reserved for the upper classes – leaders and warriors who could glean insight into how to lead and act, while also learning more about their personal lives too. Moctezuma II was reported to hold religious feasts during which mushrooms were ingested. The visions and states of intoxication were said to be advice given directly from divine beings.

CHAPTER 9

The Sixth Sun

"Let's hide deep in our hearts our love for codices, the ball game, the dances, the temples.

Let's secretly preserve the wisdom that our honourable grandparents taught us with great love,

And this knowledge will pass from parents to children, from teachers to students,

Until the rising of the Sixth Sun,

When the new wise men will bring it back and save Mexico."

Cuauhtémoc's speech, 12 August 1521

At the time of writing this book, we are right at the crest of a new Sun era. I believe this is no coincidence. As the quote above shows, it was prophesised that the knowledge of the Aztecs would be brought more fully into the open around the time of the Sixth Sun.

Each Sun era lasts for 6,625 years – and even the transitions between eras seem long in human terms. The setting of the last fifth Sun was on 26 May 2021, with the new era becoming more established by 24 November 2026.

Every era has its own distinctive characteristics and lessons. Coming out of the fifth era, we are leaving a time where the emphasis has been on what's outside us: external authorities such as religions and

Cuauhtemoc, the last Aztec ruler of Tenochtitlan, portrait from Mexican banknote

gurus, materialistic and financial status, looking outside of ourselves for answers and satisfaction.

The Sixth Sun, conversely, is a completely new era in human consciousness, in which the focus moves from the outer to the inner. Spiritual practices are essential to adapt to this shift of consciousness, and, although such practices are ancient, they are now more relevant than ever.

Learning to navigate and harmonise our internal universes has always been considered important, especially by spiritual teachers throughout different eras and cultures, but now it is fundamental – the essence of the era in which we are living. It will become increasingly difficult for those who don't adapt to this new state of being.

We will increasingly find the power, answers and healing within ourselves. The Sixth Sun is called the *Iztac Tonatiuh,* which means "the White Sun". It has been prophesised that this is the return of Quetzalcoatl – an era for people who are spiritually awakened or trained in the precious knowledge.

This is what Cuauhtémoc, the last Aztec emperor, was talking about in his speech. The Aztecs' true treasure was their knowledge and practices. With such exceptional abilities in prophecy and the calendar, they were well aware that their wisdom would be relevant to the Sixth Sun. We are living in an era of the utmost significance. The practices and the knowledge contained in this book are keys to navigating this time, and our lives, with grace and power.

Glossary

A

Acatl (aa-cat-el): Reed

Ahuacatl (aa-hwa-cat-el): Avocado

Ahuitzotl (aa-hweet-zot-el): Name of ruler

Amomati (amom-aah-ti): Black Eagle

Anahuac (aa-na-hwack): Place name

Atemoztli (atem-motz-li): Aztec month 6-25 January

Atl (atel): Water

Atlacahualo (atla-ca-hwaal-o): Aztec month 12-31 March

Axayacatl (axa-ya-caat-el) Name of ruler

Aztlan (az-tlaan) Origin place of the Aztecs

C

Cacahuatl (caca-hwaa-tel): Chocolate

Calli: House

Ce: One

Centeotl (cen-te-ot-el): The original creative force. Also known as a corn deity.

Chalchiuhuitl (chal-chi-hwee-tul): Jade

Chalchiuhtlicue (chal-chi-oo-cleek-wey): Lady of the Jade skirt

Chapultepec (chap-ool-te-pec): Place of the Grasshoppers

Chicen Itza (chi-chen itza) Mayan site

Chichimeca (chi-chi-meck-aa): Indigenous group

Chicoacen (chi-co-aa-sen): Six

Chicome (chi-co-me) Seven

Chicomecoatl (chi-co-me-co-aat-el) Goddess associated with corn

Chihuacoahuatl (chi-hwa-co-hwaa-tel): Goddess associated with tobacco

Chicuey (chi-kwaay): Eight

Chinahui (chi-na-hwee): Nine

Cipactli (chi-pact-li): Crocodile

Coatl (co-aat-el): Serpent

Coatzin (co-aa-tzin): Serpent/sexual energy

Colotl (co-lot-el): Scorpion

Cozcacuahtli (kwet-za-kwout-li): Necklace Eagle/Vulture

Cuahtli (kwout-li): Eagle

Cuauhtemoc (kwow-teh-moc): Last ruler of Tenochtitlan

Cuetzpalin (kwetz-pal-in): Lizard

Cuitlahuac (kweet-la-hwack): Moctezuma's brother

Culhuacan (cul-hwack-an): Place name

E

Etzalcualiztli (etz-al-kwal-eezt-li): month 20 June- 9 July

H

Huehyi Tecuhilhuitl (hwey-yi te-qoo-hwil-hwit-el): month 30 July- 18 August

Huehyi Tozoztli (hwey-yi tozot-zli): month 11-30 May

Huitzili (hweet-zi-li): Hummingbird

Huitzilopochtli (hweet-zi-lo-posh-tli): Hummingbird/Warrior spirit

I

Ihuitl (ee-hwit-el): Feather

Itzcuintli (its-kwint-li): Dog

Itzcoatl (its-co-aat-el): Name of place

Itzli (its-lee): Obsidian/God stone

Itzpapalotl (its-papa-lot-el): Obsidian butterfly

Izcalli: Month 15 February- 6 March

Iztac Tonatiuh (iz-tack ton-aa-tchew): Sixth Sun

M

Mahtlactli (mah-tlack-tli): Ten

Mahtlactli Omome (mah-tlack-tli om-om-me): Twelve

Mahlactli Once (mah-tlack-tli on-cey): Eleven

Mahtlactli Onyei (mahtlack-tli on-yay): Thirteen

Mah Tocuenmanahcan (ma tok-kwen-manak-can): May your intentions be planted in your dreams

Mallinalli : Twisted Ivy

Mayahuel (maya-hoo-el): Goddess

Mahcuilli (mah-quill-i): Five

Mazatl (ma-zaat-el): Deer

Metzli (metz-li): Moon

Mexicatzlin (mesh-ee-cat-zlin): dream planting exercise

Mexihca (mesh-ee-ka): Original name for Aztecs. Also refers to people who follow the Mexican dreaming traditions.

Michtlan (mich-tlan): Land of the dead

Mictecacihuatl (mick-tlan-cee-waat-el): Lady of the Underworld

Michlantecuhtli (mick-tlan-tey-koo-tli): Lord of the Underworld

Miquitzli (mi-kweetz-li): Death

Moctezuma (mock-tey-zoom-a): Ruler of the Aztec Empire

N

Nahual (nah-waal): practitioner of the tradition's spiritual practices, the dream state. Can also be an animal archetype, especially one that we become in the dream state.

Nahuatl (nah-waat-el): Indigenous Mexican language that the Toltecs and Aztecs spoke.

Nahui (naah-hwi): Four

Nemontemi: 5 days of darkness at the end of the Aztec calendar year

O

Ocelotl (o-cey-lot-el): Jaguar

Ochpaniztli (och-pan-iz-tli): Month 28 September- 17 October

Ome (om-meh): Two

Omecihuatl (om-meh-see-hwaa-tel): Mrs Two

Ometecuhtli (om-meh-tey-koot-li): Mr Two

Ometeotl (om-meh-tey-ot-el): the union of heaven and the physical world

Ollin :Movement

Ozomahtli (ozo-maah-tli): Monkey

P

Pachuha (pah-chu-ha): Name of place

Panquetzaliztli (pan-ket-zal-eez-tli): Month 17 December- 5 January

Pantli: Flag (energy centre located at the navel)

Picietl (piss-ee-et-el): Tobacco

Pipitlin (pip-it-lin): Angelic beings

Q

Quecholli (cetch-olli): Month 27 November- 16 December

Quetzal (kwet-zaal): A bird

Quetzalcoatl (Kwet-zal-co-aat-el): Feathered serpent. The essence of light, knowledge and wisdom.

Quin (kin): Protector. Physical postures.

Quiahuitl (kee-aa-weet-el): Rain

T

Tamoanchan (tamo-an-chan): Paradise

Tecpatl (teck-pat-el): Obsidian blade

Tecuhilhuitontli (tey-koo-ill-hwee-tont-li): Month 10-29 July

Tenochtitlan (ten-osh-teet-lan): Name of place

Teocuitlatl (tey-o-kwee-laat-el): Precious metals.

Teotlehco (tey-o-telck-o): Month 18 October- 6 November

Teonanacatl (teo-nana-caat-el): Psilocybin mushrooms.

Tepeilhuitl (tey-pey-hwee-tel): Month 7 November- 26 November

Tetzcoco: Name of place

Tititl (ti-ti-tel): Month 26 January- 14 February

Titocic (ti-toe-seek): Name of ruler

Tlaloc (tla-lock): He who makes things sprout

Tlacaxipehualiztli (tlack-aa-shi-pey-hwaal-eez-tli): Month 1-20 April

Tlacopan (tla-co-pan): Name of place

Tlalocan (tla-lock-can): The place of paradise

Tlatelolco (tla-tell-olk-o): Name of place

Tlav x calans (tlaz-ka-lans): Indigenous Mexican group

Tlaxochimaco (tlax-o-chi-mah-co):

Month 17 August- 7 September

Tlilxochitl (tlil-shaw-itl): Vanilla. Black flower

Tocatl (toe-cat-el): Spider

Tochtli (Tosh-tli): Rabbit

Tolpiltzen (tol-pil-tzen): A priest of Tula

Toltecayotl (tol-teck-cai-ot-el): Toltec heart

Tonal: Refers to our conscious waking state and the rational mind

Tonalli (tone-al-ee): Day glyph from the Aztec calendar

Tonalpohualli (toe-nal-po-waa-li): 260 day ritual cycle in the Aztec calendar

Topalli (top-paal-li): Sceptre

Totonalcayo (toto-nal-kai-yo): Energy centre. Heat producing spot.

Toxcatl (tox-caat-el): Month 31 May-19 June

Tozoztontli (to-zoz-tont-li): Month 21 April-10 May

Tzompantli (tzom-pant-li): Skull rack

X

Xayaxolohtli (Shay-ax-ol-oot-li): Xolotl's mask

Xictli (shick-tli): Navel

Xihuitl (she-hwee-tel): Turquoise

Xipe Totec (zi-pey to-tec): Lord of Shedding

Xiuhcoatl (she-co-at-el): Fire serpent

Xiuhpohualli (she-po-waa-li): 360 day cycle in the Aztec calendar

Xiuhtecuhtli (she-tey-coot-li): Turquoise Lord

Xochipilli (sho-shi-pill-ee): God of Flowers

Xochitl (sho-chit-el): Flower

Xocolatl (sho-co-lat-el): Bitter water. Chocolate drink.

Xocotl Huetzi (sho-cot-el wey-tzi): Month 8-27 September

Xoloitzcuintli (sho-lo-itz-kwint-li) – a breed of dog

Xolotl (sho-lot-el): God of Thunder and death

Y

Yaotl (ya-ot-el): Enemy within

Yei (ye-ee): Three

Z

Zacuan (zack-kwan): feather

Zempoalxochtli (zemp-o-al-zosh-tli): Marigold

Further Reading

BOOKS

Arredondo, Alexis A & Labrado, Eric J Magia Magia: *Invoking Mexican Magic* (Conjure South Publications 2020)

Leon-Portilla, Miguel *The Broken Spears* (Beacon Press 1962)

Magana, Sergio (Ocelocoyotl) *The Toltec Secret* (Hay House 2014)

Magana, Sergio (Ocelocoyotl) *Caves of Power* (Hay House 2016)

Magana, Sergio (Ocelocoyotl) *The Real Toltec Prophecies* (Hay House 2020)

McEwan, Colin & Lujan, Leonardo Lopez *Moctezuma: Aztec Ruler* (The British Museum Press 2009)

Rainieri, Caelum and Andersen, Ivory *The Nahualli Oracle* (Bear & Company 2003)

Townsend, Camilla *The Fifth Sun: a new history of the Aztecs* (Oxford University Press 2019)

ONLINE RESOURCES

Aztec Astrology readings:

www.warriorofthesixthsun.com

www.nematonaconnections.com

Online and in person courses. Subscribe to the mailing list for an up to date Aztec calendar count: www.sergiomagana.com